Dinner with My Daddy God

Our Divine Exchange

Joye W. Letourneau

COWCATCHER Publications

BLUFFTON, South Carolina

Copyright © 2014 by **Joye W. Letourneau**

All rights reserved. No part of this publication may be reproduced, distributed or transmitted in any form or by any means, without prior written permission.

Letourneau/COWCATCHER Publications
www.do-the-write-thing.com

Author photo by Rachel Strickland Photography.
Cover illustration by Jade of Elegant Designs.

Publisher's Note: This work is a creation of Joye W. Letourneau. All scripture quotations are from the Holy Bible, New International Version, Zondervan Bible Publishers, Grand Rapids, Michigan, USA. Copyright © 1973, 1978, 1984 by International Bible Society.

Dinner with My Daddy God/ Joye W. Letourneau. -- 1st ed.
ISBN 978-0-9960533-2-7

Joye shares many of her spiritual markers in this book, which includes her Walk to Emmaus. I first met Joye on an Emmaus journey. I experienced Jesus as she represented Him so beautifully. Years later, she continues to be the hands and feet of Christ to everyone around her. She is like Martha's sister, Mary, who chose the better thing, sitting at the feet of Jesus to be taught by Him. Like Moses, she glows from being in His presence. Many readers won't have the privilege of meeting Joye in this life; however, everyone reading this should take the opportunity to grow in faith and knowledge of Jesus Christ through her teaching. The living word has the power to set you free. May you enjoy the abundant life and your walk with Jesus.

JANICE GUGLIELMI, Savannah, GA

As you read this book, you'll feel how deep and wide God's love is. There is so much of His Spirit in this book. While reading it, I felt God's presence. Everyone who reads this book will be blessed and encouraged to enjoy a more intimate relationship with God. My husband and I plead the Blood of JESUS over each of us daily, but as a result of taking Joye's class on Communion, we recognize that healing came from His precious Body, so now we also plead the Body of JESUS over us. I believe it was absolutely God's will for her to write this book, Dinner with My Daddy God.

JAN DEVINNEY, Bluffton, SC

Joye and I have been friends for thirty-five years, which is why this book is not a surprise to me. I know how the Lord has been at work in her life and how much she loves the Word of God. I know her to be a disciplined servant of the Lord. The Lord has given my dear friend many gifts—she is so rich in HIM. I am reminded of the Samaritan woman in John 4:14 where Jesus told her the water He would give her would become a living water welling up to eternal life. I am so blessed and thankful to have her in my life. Read the book and be blessed!

PHYLLIS BROCKEL, Satellite Beach, FL

I dedicate this writing to my Daddy God.

And also to my Jesus, only because of Him do I have a relationship with my Daddy God.

I can't take credit for authoring these teachings. My knowledge comes from studying the Word of God with the Holy Spirit as my teacher. I also study the Bible teachings of many different authors. I came into this world not knowing much of anything, but I will leave this world with a considerable amount of knowledge and hopefully a little wisdom, just as each of you will.

Much of this teaching comes from the many journals I have accumulated over the years. Each day I read a chapter in the Old Testament, a chapter in the New Testament, a Psalm and a chapter in Proverbs. I also follow a daily devotional written by one of my favorite ministers. While reading, I pray and talk to the Lord as if He is right there in the room with me. When I sense Him whispering in my ear, I write down what He is saying to me.

Sometimes I do not understand what I'm studying, so I ask the Lord for the His revelation and I record His answers in my journals. Admittedly, my early journals are immature, but as I continue to grow in Christ and His Word becomes clearer, my journals have expanded. I love spending time with Him in the early morning. I cherish our daily communion and now have a deep appreciation for the Lord's desire to "dine" and have fellowship.

My Daddy God desires for each of us to grow in knowledge of Him, which is why I've written this book. Many people have encouraged me to share my teachings in writing. I will not attempt to list each person by name for fear I would leave someone out. I am indeed grateful for my supporters, my family and dear friends who have spent their valuable time reading and improving this manuscript. Thank you for lending me your eyes, ears and sharing your qualified insights.

To God be all glory and honor!

CONTENTS

Introduction 1
    HOW TO GET THE MOST FROM THIS BOOK 4
SECTION ONE   My Daddy God 7
GRACE OF GOD 7
    A Fifty-Fifty Chance 8
    God Does Not Lie 9
    Go Through 10
    Choose Healing 11
    All You Need To Know 12
DADDY GOD 15
    You Have Been Called 15
    A Man After God's Own Heart 17
    Abba Father 18
INTIMACY WITH GOD 19
    In All Four Gospels 20
    We Are His Children 23
    Ego 25
    God Knows Us 26
    Afraid of the Dark? 27
    Surrender to God's Greater Plan 28
    Consider What God Has Done 29
SECTION TWO   Our Divine Exchange 31
TWOFOLD BLESSING 31
    Have Faith for Both 32
    Beware of Satan's Counterfeits 34

THE BREAD OF HEAVEN 37
    First Reference 38
    Passover 39
    The Significance of Breaking the Bread 41
    Understanding the Bread 43
    The Passover Seder Connection 46

THIS IS MY BODY 49
    The Bread of Life 49
    Twofold Cure 51
    Healing is the Children's Bread 53
    Faith Rewarded 54
    Jesus, The Healer 55
    Take a Stand 56
    The Power of Belief 57
    The Bible 58
    The Woman with the Issue of Blood 60
    Miraculous Healing 62
    Maturity in Christ 63
    The Most Significant Story Ever Told 64
    Use Words Wisely 65

THIS IS MY BLOOD 69
    The New Covenant 70
    The Final Sacrifice 71
    Jesus is Your Shield 73
    The Veil is Gone, the Curtain is Open 75
    Life in the Blood 77
    Forgiveness, the Healing Balm 77
    The One Thing 78
    Your Full Potential is in God 82
    The Benefits of Forgiveness 83

  Forgiveness is a Choice 85
  Confidence in Prayer 88
  Power of Proclaiming 89
TAKING COMMUNION 91
  Anywhere, Anytime 91
  Is it Just a Piece of Bread? 92
  Order 94
  Taking Communion in an Unworthy Manner 96
  Him Alone 97
  What Does it Mean to Drink Judgment? 98
  The Meaning of Salvation 100
  Keep His Word 101
  Righteousness is a Gift 102
SECTION THREE His Divine Plan 105
OUR GREAT JOY 105
  Finished Work Prophesied 106
  The Vine 107
  The New Wine 109
  Bruising and Breaking 111
  Freedom, Joy, Restoration 113
  Bible Study 114
  Perseverance 115
FORGIVENESS 117
  Obedience 117
  Forgiveness for Your Sake 118
  Don't Grow Weary 119
SUFFERING 121
  No Tear is Wasted 121
  Enemy Attacks 122
  Shattered Dreams 123

IN HIS PRESENCE 125
   Priorities 125
   Flow in God's Power 127
   You are His Presence in the World 129
   Spiritual Retreats 131
   Walk to Emmaus 131
   What Happened on the Road to Emmaus? 132
   My Prayer for You 135
FINAL THOUGHTS 137
   Daddy God Really Is… 137
EPILOGUE 141

Introduction

My mission in writing this book is to unveil the beauty of the Body and Blood of Jesus and what His finished work provided. But before you begin reading, please pray with me.

God, open our eyes to see and our ears to hear from you. Give us your revelation knowledge and wisdom of you as only you can. Amen!

Let's start with a few questions.

Have you been robbed of an important avenue of healing and wholeness in your life?

Have you not taken the Lord's Supper because you thought it would cause God's judgment to fall on you?

Did you believe you had to be prayed up, confessed up and living a perfect life prior to partaking?

Did you try to make everything right before receiving the elements?

Did you just simply give up because you thought it was easier not to partake?

If you answered yes to any of these questions, you should know that these ideas are lies straight from the devil. They do not resemble the teachings found in God's Word. Yes, indeed, we have been robbed. There is absolutely nothing the devil fears more than the Bread and the Cup in the hands of a believer who really understands and lives this revelation.

Did you know that when you come to His Table, you receive the Body and the Blood to receive the divine life of Jesus? Holy Communion is a blessing when you release your faith to receive what Jesus died to give you. The loving heart of God is expressed in Communion. It is not a ritual but a blessing in which you participate. As you celebrate and release your faith in His finished work, you are doing so "in remembrance of Him."

When you drink the wine, you are reminded that His Blood, the Blood of the sinless Son of God, did not just bring forgiveness to you, but that His Blood also made you forever righteous, holy and blameless in the sight of God. His pure Blood has covered your unrighteousness completely.

When you place your trust in Him, know that you are forgiven for any past, present and future sins. The moment you place that trust in Him, you are the righteousness of God in Christ Jesus. When you eat the Bread and drink the Wine, you are reminded of His finished work.

Today, as a believer, you are in perfect standing with the Father. His ears are attentive to your voice. He is your High Priest and has sprinkled His Blood on the true mercy seat in heaven. Because of His perfect sacrifice, you are in perfect standing before Him—forever. He listens when you pray.

You can celebrate during communion because He wants to commune *with* you. He hears and answers your prayers.

Revelation 3:20 *Here I am! I stand at the door and knock. If anyone hears my voice and opens the door, I will come in and eat with that person, and they with me.*

The Greek word for "to eat" (or to dine or have dinner) is *deipnon*. In the days of Jesus, it was the main meal of the day. It was a leisurely affair. The meal is never rushed, which speaks to the depth of His invitation and desire for relationship.

Jesus desires to dine with you. It is not merely a quick visit. He desires to sit and spend time fellowshipping with you. This type of dining allows you to receive more of His wisdom, knowledge and understanding. Consider it an honor to dine with Him and feed on His Word.

The Body and the Blood of Jesus—we do this in remembrance of Him. The Body is for healing and the Blood is for forgiveness. Rest in the finished work of Jesus by coming to His table to partake of the Holy Communion.

Receive restoration and wholeness.

HOW TO GET THE MOST FROM THIS BOOK

This book has three distinct sections. You may choose to read the book in order, front to back, or you may choose to skip around. Let the Holy Spirit be your guide.

The first section offers readers an understanding of my Daddy God. I describe what intimacy with God looks like and how to express our faith in Him.

The second section explains the divine exchange that occurs during Holy Communion. It is important for the body of Christ to gain a full revelation of the Lord's Supper. After reading this section, you will have a deeper understanding of the Bread and the Wine, the Body and the Blood. This is where readers will receive a deeper revelation of God's twofold blessing—healing and forgiveness.

The third section covers God's divine plan for His children. My hope is that these topics will inspire you to spend time with God so you can dwell in His presence continually.

I conclude with an epilogue. I wanted readers to have at their disposal a simple rendition of the prayer of salvation as well as the prayer often used while taking communion.

Now it's my turn to pray for you.

I pray that your fears will be far removed when you come to His Table to receive health and wholeness through His Body and His Blood. May God richly bless you in every imaginable way with His favor, grace and great love.

SECTION ONE

MY DADDY GOD

I don't just believe God is real, I know He is.

—Joye W. Letourneau

GRACE OF GOD

I would not, and could not have written this book if it were not for the GRACE of God in my life. Let me explain.

In June, of 1999 I was diagnosed with cancer. My diagnosis was found during a routine physical with my physician. Suddenly my full calendar for the upcoming days and weeks became insignificant. My life changed drastically. The "C" word took me on an unexpected journey. To this day, I still refer to it as the "C" word.

My mother died of the "C" word when I was only nine years old. Mama had been sick since I was five. In fact, she spent the last two years of her life in hospitals, only coming home for occasional weekend visits. I really did not want to put my family through such a difficult ordeal. Because of my firsthand experience with the disease, I had to be convinced to take the treatments. I knew what it could do to a family.

A Fifty-Fifty Chance

The doctors gave me a 50% chance of recovery, which meant they really didn't know whether I would, or wouldn't, outlive the disease. My son, Mike, insisted I take the treatments. He wanted me to take the treatments that I knew were so horrific and I was so much against. He was pulling at my very heartstrings.

I asked myself, "Am I being selfish for not wanting to go through all of this?" The honest answer was no. I can honestly say that I did not give myself any consideration. I did not want *him* to have to go through this dreadful and frightful experience, which I knew he would have to do when I took the treatments. Mike won. And I thank God we fought that battle. Fifteen years later, I'm here and healthy. I am also eager to discuss my experience and share my journey.

As prescribed, treatments were scheduled immediately after surgery. The surgeon couldn't remove 100% of my affected lymph nodes, so after the malignant tumor was removed, I was prescribed radiation therapy. Radiation, they said, would improve my odds for a full recovery. In fact, I had radiation therapy and chemotherapy simultaneously.

Treatment was tough to get through. Chemotherapy lasted much longer than the radiation, and although it did get better, it was still a long and difficult road. My body received radiation five days a week for six weeks. I received chemotherapy five days a week for eleven months. To allow my body to recoup from all the poison that had been pumped into my system, I was given one week off from chemotherapy each month.

I used the hours it took to complete my chemotherapy to listen to healing scriptures on CDs. I claimed my healing and constantly thanked God for it. The Word of God is the foundation of faith, and because of the time I spent in His holy presence, my heart was purified.

God Does Not Lie

Words can't begin to describe the tremendous strength and comfort I gained from God's Word. God keeps His promises; He cannot lie.

My admonition to everyone reading this is to stand on God's promises and say to yourself what He says about you in His Word. We must know His promises so that when trials come, we can ask for His help. He will not fail us. It is our lack of knowledge of God and His Word that prevents us from receiving the many blessings He has promised.

Hosea 4:6 *...my people are destroyed from lack of knowledge.*

In our own strength, we are no match for most of life's problems. That's why we must learn to depend on the power and wisdom of God and His Word. When we hide God's promises in our heart, they will be with us to comfort and strengthen us during precarious and difficult times. Do you know that our prayers are made much more effective by our knowledge of God's promises found in His written Word?

Throughout my difficult time, God gave me this Scripture. It is still my favorite verse.

Isaiah 43:1-2 *Do not fear, for I have redeemed you; I have called you by name; you are mine! When you pass through the waters (chemotherapy), I will be with you; and through the rivers, they shall not overflow you. When you walk through the fire (radiation), you shall not be burned, nor shall the flames scorch you.*

For me, "the waters" represented chemotherapy. The drugs given to me were clear and looked just like water. "The fire" represented radiation. Radiation's nuclear particles (or rays of heat) are produced by overexposure to radioactive matter, which is very destructive, fire-like destructive.

Go Through

With this Scripture and God's grace, I walked *through* the "C" word! I made a partnership with God and took one day at a time. I've been *through* the water and I've been *through* the fire, and I thank the Lord. His blood has cleansed and purified me.

Psalm 23 says it in another way:

The LORD is my shepherd, I shall not be in want. He makes me lie down in green pastures, he leads me beside quiet waters, he restores my soul. He guides me in paths of righteousness for his name's sake. Even though I walk through the valley of the shadow of death, I will fear no evil, for you are with me; your rod and your staff, they comfort me.
You prepare a table before me in the presence of my enemies. You anoint my head with oil; my cup overflows. Surely goodness and love will follow me all the days of my life, and I will dwell in the house of the LORD forever.

Verse 6 in the Hebrew translation literally says, "Surely goodness and mercy shall hunt me down all the days of my life." Imagine God's goodness and mercy aggressively hunting you down and overtaking you every day, every moment and everywhere until there's simply no way for you to escape the blessing of God!

God said we would walk in the *valley* of the shadow of death, but He also said we wouldn't *stay* there. He said that we would walk **through the valley**. Let Psalm 23 speak to your heart in a fresh way about the kindness and loving care God wants to give you.

Choose Healing

Choose healing. The more you understand the truth of those words, the more you will be able to trust God no matter what situation you face in life. Your confidence in Him will make you bold.

As I said, I boldly claimed the Word of God and His promises during my illness. My sick body lined up with the Word of God. I chose to be healed, just as I chose to be saved. For me, it was a faith thing. I don't just understand the goodness of God; I have seen it work in my life.

After several years of being cancer free, the radiation oncologist asked me, "What do you think was the secret to maintaining your healing when others had not?"

My answer, "I can't speak for others, but I believe my healing was the result of my strong faith in a God that desires me to be whole and healthy."

It was this conversation that encouraged me to begin seeking the Lord and the scriptures to get a better understanding of healing. This eventually led to a study on the Lord's Supper. I was honored and privileged to teach this at my church. I taught the class for a year and received more and more revelation as time went on, after which, I felt compelled to write this book about Communion.

All You Need To Know

I read a story some time ago about a Sunday School teacher who was teaching her young class to memorize the twenty-third Psalm. She gave the youngsters a month to learn the six verses. One little boy was excited about the task but just couldn't remember the Psalm. After much practice, he could barely get past the first line.

On the day they were scheduled to recite Psalm 23 in front of the congregation, the little boy was so nervous. When it was his turn, he stepped up to the microphone and said proudly, 'The Lord is my Shepherd and that's all I need to know!"

How profound is that? What can we take away from this little boy's simplistic faith? Everything we need to know. *The Lord is my Shepherd, and that's all I need to know.*

End of story.

DADDY GOD

"If God is for us, who can be against us?"

—**Romans 8: 31**

I have found that praising God each day for who He is raises me above my circumstances. I know Jesus Christ is greater than my pain. He promised in His Word that His grace would be sufficient. Since His Words are true, they will hold up under any and all kinds of painful circumstances.

When you meet with Him, in the throne room of your heart, you will not walk away empty. Tell Him how wonderful, in counsel, and magnificent, in wisdom, He is. Submit all your gifts and stand under His authority that He gives you. You are made to be more than a conqueror through His Spirit inside of you. Let Him bring forth that which is life around you.

You Have Been Called

He has placed a call upon your life and one that cannot be hindered, which is why you must cast out everything that tries to tell you to give up on your dreams and visions. His Spirit rules and reigns in you. He flows out of you with great discernment and knowledge. Always take Him with you wherever you go.

Seek God to equip and encourage you to do the right thing in all circumstances. After doing that, don't allow obstacles to prevent you from moving forward in life. Break *through* obstacles and bloom gloriously wherever you are planted. Draw near to Him and be faithful. God is the focus that provides confidence and conviction and moves us forward, regardless of circumstances.

Romans 8:31 *What, then, shall we say in response to these things? If God is for us, who can be against us?*

You can rest assured that the prince of darkness will bow his knee and with his tongue acknowledge that Jesus Christ is Lord, to the glory of God, your Daddy God.

Philippians 2:9-11 *Therefore God exalted him to the highest place and gave him the name that is above every name, that at the name of Jesus every knee should bow, in heaven and on earth and under the earth, and every tongue acknowledge that Jesus Christ is Lord, to the glory of God the Father.*

Romans 14:11 *It is written: "'As surely as I live,' says the Lord, 'every knee will bow before me; every tongue will confess to God.'"*

Romans 8:15 *For you did not receive a spirit that makes you a slave again to fear, but you received the Spirit of sonship. And by him we cry, Abba Father.*

A Man After God's Own Heart

God called David a man after His own heart. While tending his flock of sheep on the hills of Israel, David fellowshipped with God. He came to know God's nature. He acknowledged that the Lord was *his* Shepherd. David knew God was a loving God, good, kind and patient. He knew God would take care of him, provide for him and deliver him from danger. As David became aware of God's goodness, he wrote Psalm 23, revealing what God wants to do for us here on earth.

I believe David experienced the more abundant life spoken of in the New Testament. It is the doctrine of supplying our desires as well as our needs. Using the words, "I shall not want," David was saying he knew God was guiding him in ways that caused him to be secure and prosperous.

For David, the word **through** meant safe passage.

Through the valley of the shadow of death—the deep, waterless, gloomy, wild beast-infested, rocky, dangerous, death-lurking ravine common in Palestine. David had no fear of evil because of the Shepherd's constant companionship and watchful protection.

Comfort came from the Shepherd's rod (the club) and staff (the crook), the only two things carried by shepherds for defense and protection. The club was for the sheep's enemies and the crook for the sheep's protection when they strayed. The sheep feasted in safety while the Shepherd watched, fought and protected them. God does the same for each one of us.

What a description of Abba Father, our Daddy God!

Abba Father

In Scripture there are many different names used to describe God. While all the names of God are important in many ways, the name "Abba Father" is one of the most significant names of God in understanding how He relates to people. The word *Abba* is an Aramaic word that would most closely be translated as "Daddy." It was a common term that young children would use to address their fathers. It signifies the close, intimate relationship of a father to his child, as well as the childlike trust that a young child puts in his daddy.

Your Daddy God is right in the midst of your struggles, and challenges. His super abounding grace is all around you, forgiving you, hearing you, providing for you and transforming your weaknesses into strengths. Go to His Word to see your situation as He sees it, and then anchor your thoughts and emotions onto His unshakable Word.

Choose to believe what the Word say about you and your situation. He is transforming you from the inside out.

He is your Cornerstone.

INTIMACY WITH GOD

To fall in love with God is the greatest of all romances; To seek Him, the greatest adventure; To find him, the greatest human achievement.

—Augustine

The Greek word for communion is *koinonia*. It means intimacy, or fellowship.

Intimacy flourishes and produces a confident expectation when obedience comes from the heart, not the mind. In other words, Holy Communion is not some magical formula to obey to get right with God. Communion should be a mindful and heart-felt decision. Communion is intimate and personal.

And here's why. In every miracle that Christ performed, the person's healing was always linked to their faith. Christ does not force healing on anyone. He is always a gentleman. In the same respect, Christ does not force salvation. Holy Spirit is the one who woos us into recognizing the love of Jesus. Holy Spirit makes the love of Christ real to us. He gives us revelation, understanding and wisdom. He teaches us, as a private tutor would offer customized and personal instruction. Yes, it's very personal.

So when you take Communion, you should meditate on the finished work of Christ. You must recognize that He suffered for you. Because He died and was resurrected from the grave, you can enjoy the atonement that His goodness, mercy and grace provided. Take it personally!

In All Four Gospels

The Lord's Supper is so important that accounts of it are found in all four gospels, all of which include the powerful truth of the Lord's Supper. Read for yourself:

Matthew 26:17-19 *On the first day of the Feast of Unleavened Bread, the disciples came to Jesus and asked, "Where do you want us to make preparations for you to eat the Passover?"*
He replied, "Go into the city to a certain man and tell him, 'The Teacher says: My appointed time is near. I am going to celebrate the Passover with my disciples at your house.'" So the disciples did as Jesus had directed them and prepared the Passover.

Matthew 26: 26-29 *While they were eating, Jesus took bread, gave thanks and broke it, and gave it to his disciples, saying, "Take and eat; this is my body."*
Then he took the cup, gave thanks and offered it to them, saying, "Drink from it, all of you. This is my blood of the covenant, which is poured out for many for the forgiveness of sins. I tell you, I will not drink of this fruit of the vine from now on until that day when I drink it anew with you in my Father's kingdom."

Mark 14:17-25 *When evening came, Jesus arrived with the Twelve. While they were reclining at the table eating, he said, "Truly I tell you, one of you will betray me—one who is eating with me."*

They were saddened, and one by one they said to him, "Surely you don't mean me?"

"It is one of the Twelve," he replied, "one who dips bread into the bowl with me. The Son of Man will go just as it is written about him. But woe to that man who betrays the Son of Man! It would be better for him if he had not been born."

While they were eating, Jesus took bread, gave thanks broke it, and gave it to his disciples, saying, "Take it; this is my body."

Then he took the cup, gave thanks and offered it to them, and they all drank from it.

"This is my blood of the covenant, which is poured out for many," he said to them. "I tell you the truth, I will not drink again of the fruit of the vine until that day when I drink it anew in the kingdom of God."

Luke 22:7-22 *Then came the day of Unleavened Bread on which the Passover lamb had to be sacrificed. Jesus sent Peter and John, saying, "Go and make preparations for us to eat the Passover."*

"Where do you want us to prepare for it?" they asked.

He replied, "As you enter the city, a man carrying a jar of water will meet you. Follow him to the house that he enters, [11] *and say to the owner of the house, 'The Teacher asks: Where is the guest room, where I may eat the Passover with my disciples?' He will show you a large upper room, all furnished. Make preparations there."*

They left and found things just as Jesus had told them. So they prepared the Passover.

When the hour came, Jesus and his apostles reclined at the table. And he said to them, "I have eagerly desired to eat this Passover with you before I suffer. For I tell you, I will not eat it again until it finds fulfillment in the kingdom of God."

After taking the cup, he gave thanks and said, "Take this and divide it among you. For I tell you I will not drink again of the fruit of the vine until the kingdom of God comes."

And he took bread, gave thanks and broke it, and gave it to them, saying, "This is my body given for you; do this in remembrance of me."

In the same way, after the supper he took the cup, saying, "This cup is the new covenant in my blood, which is poured out for you. But the hand of him who is going to betray me is with mine on the table. The Son of Man will go as it has been decreed. But woe to that man who betrays him."

John 13:21-30 *After he had said this, Jesus was troubled in spirit and testified, "I tell you the truth, one of you is going to betray me."*

His disciples stared at one another, at a loss to know which of them he meant. One of them, the disciple whom Jesus loved, was reclining next to him. Simon Peter motioned to this disciple and said, "Ask him which one he means."

Leaning back against Jesus, he asked him, "Lord, who is it?"

Jesus answered, "It is the one to whom I will give this piece of bread when I have dipped it in the dish." Then, dipping the piece of bread, he gave it to Judas Iscariot, son of Simon. As soon as Judas took the bread, Satan entered into him.

"What you are about to do, do quickly," Jesus told him, but no one at the meal understood why Jesus said this to him. Since Judas had charge of the money, some thought Jesus was telling him to buy what was needed for the Feast, or to give something to the poor. As soon as Judas had taken the bread, he went out. And it was night.

There you have it—from the last Passover meal Jesus shared with His disciples to Judas' betrayal. Rejoice! Because all of it leads up to the death, burial and resurrection of Jesus—God's plan for man's redemption!

We Are His Children

He is our Father God. We are His children, forever related to Him through the Blood and Body of Jesus. We are not merely introduced to God by Jesus Christ for a friendly interview, but we are to remain with Him as part of His household. As His children, we are like silver and gold when refined. He grants us grace to endure trials without sustaining loss or deterioration.

Zechariah 9: 13 *"This third I will bring into the fire; I will refine them like silver and test them like gold. They will call upon my name and I will answer them; I will say, 'They are my people, and they will say, 'The LORD is our God.'"*

Understand, that while you will have fears, doubts, and difficulties, you can still trust God. In fact, the Bible teaches us that, no matter what our circumstances may be, we can and should trust and rely on Him more than we trust and rely on our own understanding.

Proverbs 3:5-8 *Trust in the LORD with all your heart and lean not on your own understanding; in all your ways acknowledge him, and he will make your paths straight. Do not be wise in your own eyes; fear the LORD and shun evil. This will bring health to your body and nourishment to your bones.*

Sometimes our troubles overshadow our view of God. When the pressure is on, we tend to question our faith in God. The things we felt absolutely sure of in the good times are suddenly overlooked. However, God has not left us, nor will

He ever leave us. We must trust God in the midst of our agony.

The key is to take time to pray for God's guidance in the midst of your circumstances. Allow Him the freedom to speak to you through His Word.

Romans 5:1-5 *Therefore, since we have been justified through faith, we have peace with God through our Lord Jesus Christ, through whom we have gained access by faith into this grace in which we now stand. And we rejoice in the hope of the glory of God. Not only so, but we also glory in our sufferings, because we know that suffering produces perseverance; perseverance, character; and character, hope. And hope does not disappoint us, because God has poured out his love into our hearts by the Holy Spirit, whom has been given to us.*

Psalm 36: 5-6 *Your love, O LORD, reaches to the heavens, your faithfulness to the skies. Your righteousness is like the mighty mountains, your justice like the great deep. O LORD, you preserve both man and beast.*

Psalm 103:11 -12 *For as high as the heavens are above the earth, so great is his love for those who fear him; as far as the east is from the west, so far has he removed our transgressions from us.*

Romans 8: 35, 37-39 *Who shall separate us from the love of Christ? Shall trouble or hardship or persecution or famine or nakedness or danger or sword?*
    No, in all these things we are more than conquerors through him who loved us. For I am convinced that neither death nor life, neither angels nor demons, neither the present nor the future, nor any powers, neither height nor depth, nor anything else in all creation, will be able to separate us from the love of God that is in Christ Jesus our Lord.

Remember, the love, mercy and grace found in the blue of heaven is bigger than all the clouds in the sky.

Ego

The most satisfying feeling you can experience is to be alone with God in His presence. When you continue to do what you know is wrong, you will eventually become corrupted and unable to feel His presence. To redirect your thoughts and actions, you must be honest with yourself and God. You need to be *totally* honest with yourself and God. Check your ego at the door and be alone with God. He tells us to be still and know that He is God. But in order to hear God's voice, our ego must be quiet.

Psalm 46:10 *Be still, and know that I am God; I will be exalted among the nations, I will be exalted in the earth.*

It takes courage to listen to God with a totally honest heart. It takes even greater courage to *follow through* when we hear from God. Even though daily circumstances will bombard us with noise and others will pressure us into making decisions, it's important to hear God's whisper.

Isaiah 58:11 *The Lord will guide you always; he will satisfy your needs in a sun-scorched land and will strengthen your frame. You will be like a well-watered garden, like a spring whose waters never fail.*

God replenishes our spirits and renews our strength. He will sustain us in all circumstances. Face the challenge and rebuild your life with God's help. Your needs will be supplied in times of drought and disaster. Don't allow the voice of your ego to get in the way of God's voice.

God Knows Us

God's knowledge of us is intimate. Read and consider how the psalmist put it.

Psalm 139: 1-10 *O LORD, you have searched me, Lord, and you know me. You know when I sit and when I rise; you perceive my thoughts from afar. You discern my going out and my lying down; you are familiar with all my ways. Before a word is on my tongue you know it completely, O LORD.*
You hem me in—behind and before; you have laid your hand upon me. Such knowledge is too wonderful for me, too lofty for me to attain.
Where can I go from your Spirit? Where can I flee from your presence? If I go up to the heavens, you are there; if I make my bed in the depths, you are there. If I rise on the wings of the dawn, if I settle on the far side of the sea, your right hand will guide me, your right hand will hold me fast.

Did you notice that God operates in heaven and on earth? *If I go up to the heavens, you are there... If I rise on the wings of the dawn, if I settle on the far side of the sea, even there your hand will guide me, your right hand will hold me fast.*

God's presence is felt in all parts of the universe. No man can escape His presence.

Afraid of the Dark?

But where is God when it is dark? There are times in our lives when darkness overwhelms us. We feel lost and alone; we are afraid God cannot find us. How thankful we should be that this is not true. When the darkness engulfs us, it does not engulf God. For God, the night is as bright as a sunshiny day.

God brings forth light in order to release us from all the darkness that keeps us in old, destructive cycles. Do not get stuck in self-condemnation, guilt, shame or unending grief. You can't allow your emotions to rule or allow the enemy to lie. Never let the enemy dictate who you are.

To the Lord, the night is as bright as the day. And what's more, God invites us to share the experience of being led out of the darkness into the light of life. When we experience darkness, light becomes more radiant. With God's help, the darkness will be less dark and the depths of misery will be not as miserable. With God, each day will carry with it something to celebrate.

Psalm 139: 11-12 *If I say, "Surely the darkness will hide me and the light become night around me," even the darkness will not be dark to you; the night will shine like the day, for darkness is as light to you.*

Ephesians 5:8 *For you were once darkness, but now you are light in the Lord.*

For this reason and many more, you can rejoice!

Surrender to God's Greater Plan

When you feel stuck, or slowed down by pain, trials or tribulations, remember God has a bigger and better plan than what you are experiencing at the moment. Welcome the fact that God doesn't see you through your eyes; He sees you through His Holy eyes. Once you properly understand God's image of you, you can begin to see your life from a different perspective.

In other words, look beyond the natural provisions of this world to His heavenly provisions. Trust Him for more than what appears to be true in your natural eyes. If you think about God's provisions, there is much more for you than against you, and that fact alone should bring peace far beyond your understanding. Open your eyes to see His ever-present answer(s) for you.

Develop greater levels of obedience. Do what God's Word says to do. Respond to your enemies with God's loving kindness and compassion, even and especially those who have hurt you deeply. Place your enemies at His mercy and learn to bless instead of curse. You are not of this world. You cannot respond in the spirit of this world. God is love so you must respond in the power of His might.

Satan had a plan to surround me with darkness. He offered me hopelessness. He wanted to steal my bright future and destroy my dreams. But God had a greater plan. At the moment, when my life seemed to be hanging in the balance, I chose Christ even though I was hurt, humiliated, weakened and falling into Satan's plan.

Consider What God Has Done

I submitted to the truth of God's Word and God took me to heights far exceeding the depths that I had experienced during my time of trials. God was able to straighten what Satan intended to make crooked. Praise God!

Ecclesiastes 7:13-14 *Consider what God has done: Who can straighten what he has made crooked? When times are good, be happy; but when times are bad, consider this: God has made the one as well as the other. Therefore, a man cannot discover anything about their future.*

When I surrendered to Christ, it was not a defeat but a victory over the circumstances I had been trying to control. Not being in control is actually liberating. We tend to hide our weaknesses, which puts us in bondage to the weakness. Allowing God to be in control and sharing in God's strength produces freedom.

Did you know that Christ empowers you to trust Him no matter what you are going through? Trust Him that you are going to go **THROUGH** *whatever* you're going through. Remember His plan. Your circumstance is a part of a much larger plan that will bear fruit in the proper time. God sees what we can't. God wastes nothing; He uses everything for His plan.

God did not call us to be victims of circumstances. He calls us to grow closer to Him by courageously working through our dilemmas. When we pour out all the bitter waters that well up in our hearts, we allow God to pour living sweet water back in those empty holes. Only God's love can fill an empty hole or void in your life.

God loves you and has a purpose for your life. He wants you to succeed and prosper and serve as a model to help others.

Jeremiah 29:11 *"For I know the plans I have for you," declares the Lord, "plans to prosper you and not to harm you, plans to give you hope and a future.*

Praise God!

SECTION TWO

OUR DIVINE EXCHANGE

The greatest miracle in our lives is our salvation, which we get by the grace of God. Our life in Jesus is not started from the questions, "What have I done?" but "what He has done?" The true message of the Gospel is, in fact, centered on a unique and extraordinary event that happened only once in history—when Jesus died on the cross to be the atoning sacrifice for mankind.

—Derek Prince

TWOFOLD BLESSING

I was taught the two elements were lumped together and that both were for forgiveness of sins, when in reality, it is *two* applications. There are two elements to the Lord's Supper because there is a two-fold application.

Have Faith for Both

I heard a story once where a pastor who believed strongly in salvation but was questioning healing.

A minister questioned his friend, a pastor. "If you believe in healing so strongly, why didn't you go to the hospitals and heal all the sick?"

The pastor replied, "Tell me…why didn't you go to the hospital and get them all saved?"

The minister said, "You have to believe in order to be saved."

And the pastor said, "A person must believe in order to be healed!"

Communion is so powerful because it is your own personal faith in God's covenant. God is true to His Word. He loves to see you act on your faith. He loves it when you understand His covenant. And did you know that when we walk with God under His new covenant, we are in line with God's will?

Psalm 89:34 *I will not violate my covenant or alter what my lips have uttered.*

Have you ever heard or said, "I plead the Blood of Jesus over _____*(fill in the blank with anything)*_____?" But my question is, have you ever heard or said, "I plead the Body of Jesus?"

Communion is twofold—salvation from sin and healing from sickness. The wine is His Blood and is for your forgiveness. The Bread is His Body and is for your healing. The provision is for both, which means there is something wrong when we take the Bread and deny that healing is for today. If you do this, you negate half of what Christ did on the Cross.

The Two-Fold Blessing
Body of Christ – for healing
Blood of Christ – for forgiveness

We begin with God's first fold blessing—forgiveness. From a vertical perspective, we are reminded of God above and His forgiveness toward us below. From the horizontal perspective, we are reminded to have forgiveness for each other.

God's second fold blessing is healing. From the vertical view, we are reminded that healing comes down to us from God through Jesus. From the horizontal perspective, we are reminded to minister the life of God to each other.

Have you ever noticed that our relationship with God and His Word is vertically oriented, and that our relationship with men is horizontally oriented? Then take a look and see how, when connected, these two relationships form a cross.

Beware of Satan's Counterfeits

Satan has a counterfeit to God's mercy, grace and blessings. His counterfeits are twofold as well. His first fold begins with sin and is designed to tear down our relationship with God. Satan's second fold is sickness, designed to kill and destroy our bodies. Do not be deceived; Satan wants us to be totally broken.

But God's twofold blessing exchanges (or replaces) these two evils with abundant life. God blesses you not because you are good, but because He is good!

Jesus shed His Blood not only for the remission of our sins, but he also *put away* our sicknesses and our infirmities. The word for "put away" means to lock in, or to consign to a place where it cannot escape or be removed. Jesus' Body put your sicknesses and infirmities away. They are locked away, removed from your position. This is what you must discern when you are remembering His Body.

Knowing what His Body did for you—that is what is referred to as "discerning His Body." Most believers understand how to discern the Blood, but many do not know how to discern the Lord's Body. After reading this, I hope the two applications of the Lord's Supper are instantly recognizable.

THE BREAD OF HEAVEN

We will not have the spiritual maturity necessary to weather life's storms successfully by sitting in our "tents" and hoping that we will somehow make it through this difficult season. God gives us the choice to go out and gather what He feeds us. It behooves us to feast on the Bread of Life—JESUS CHRIST—daily.

—Billy Graham

Like the Israelites, we must go out and gather our daily bread—straight from the Word of God.

Exodus 16:4 *Then the Lord said to Moses, "Behold, I will rain bread from heaven for you; and the people shall go out and gather a day's portion every day, that I may test them, whether or not they will walk in my instructions."*

Notice that God did not say He would have this bread delivered straight to their tents. He said the people were to go out and gather the daily bread from heaven. Likewise, when hard times come, we can greatly benefit from the foundation laid in our hearts by spending time studying the Bible and praying on a daily basis.

Did you know that the first reference to the use of bread and wine occurs in the Old Testament? It takes place when

Abraham met Melchizedek in Jerusalem. Melchizedek was noted to be the first king and priest of the Most High God.

First Reference

The story begins with Abram and his army of servants and allies defeating an invading army. They rescued the people and possessions of Sodom, his nephew Lot among them. After the surprising victory, Melchizedek appears on the scene with bread, wine and a blessing.

Genesis14:18-20 *Then Melchizedek king of Salem brought out bread and wine. He was priest of God Most High, and he blessed Abram, saying, "Blessed be Abram by God Most High, Creator of heaven and earth. And blessed be God Most High who delivered your enemies into your hand."*

Melchizedek brought bread and wine, the same elements we use in the Lord's Supper. The Lord's Supper is a blessing Jesus brings to us. He blesses us through the meal that He shares with us. In the same way, Melchizedek brought bread and wine and then blessed Abram. The blessing and the meal, after all, is Christ's idea. It is His ordinance for His church. He tells us that the elements are His Body and His Blood and we should remember Him as we consume the elements.

The first time God sent His people bread from heaven was when He sent manna to Israelites as they wandered through the desert.

John 6:32 *"I tell you the truth, it is not Moses who has given you the bread from heaven, but it is my Father who gives you the true bread from heaven."*

Exodus 16:15 *When the Israelites saw it, they said to each other, "What is it?" For they did not know what it was. Moses said to them, "It is the bread the LORD has given you to eat."*

They had never seen manna before so Moses had explained it to them, "It is the bread the Lord has given you to eat." The manna represented salvation, however, it was not the true Bread of heaven, which is Jesus Christ. When Christ came, Israel again asked for an explanation. "Who is He?" they asked.

Just as manna was eaten daily, we also can partake of the true Bread of heaven daily, through Communion. The Bread is a picture of Christ's Body. Participating in the Lord's Supper is a wonderful honor, and the Communion meal is where believers in Christ enjoy the privilege of fellowshipping with the Lord.

Passover

Religious Jews honor the ancient Passover each year as they remember their night of deliverance from Egyptian slavery. However, Jesus introduced a new covenant at the Last Supper. His own Body and Blood would seal the new covenant. Passover would no longer signify freedom from Egyptian slavery. Believers in Christ would celebrate (and remember) their deliverance from sin, sickness, and the power of Satan!

Matthew 26: 19 *So the disciples did as Jesus had directed them and prepared the Passover.*

Reflect on this for a moment: Each time you lift the cup of Communion to your mouth to receive the Bread and Blood of Communion, you are to remember your past deliverance from the penalty of sin, your present deliverance from the power of sin, and your future redemption from the presence of sin.

Every believer should recognize the historical application of Passover and see the prophetic fulfillment in Christ who died to take the place of God's final sacrificial Lamb. Just as the Jewish Passover reminded Hebrews of their promised land, communion is a reminder of the Christian's redemption through Christ's suffering. It is also a reminder of our future inheritance with Christ in heaven.

Did you know that *shalom* in Hebrew is defined as wholeness, health, prosperity and peace? And now we know, the Body and the Blood of God's lamb brought complete healing, redemption and prosperity and peace. The wounds and stripes on Christ's body brought healing and salvation. It is through Christ's blood on the cross that God delivers and redeems us.

Communion is a sign of our belief in Christ's finished work and a testimony of our faith in the complete work of salvation. Shalom!

The Significance of Breaking the Bread

Many believers in the church do not understand the significance of the breaking of bread during Communion. Yet God has ordained the Holy Communion as a solution for disease and sickness. Jesus' body had to be broken so that when God's people come to His Table, they will recognize (and remember) that Holy Communion *is* God's channel for divine health. There is power in the Lord's broken Body—power to bring health to our bodies when we come to His table. When you eat the Bread, you are receiving the divine life of Jesus, which entitles you to walk in good health and wholeness.

The early church believed this.

Acts 2:42 *They devoted themselves to the apostles' teaching and to fellowship, to the breaking of bread and prayer.*

Most believers understand the importance of doctrine, fellowship and prayer but few truly understand the significance of the breaking of bread. Next to salvation, divine health is the greatest blessing we can receive. Scripture explains why believers are weak and sick and die prematurely.

1 Corinthians 11:29-30 *For anyone who eats and drinks without recognizing the body of the Lord eats and drinks judgment on himself. That is why many among you are weak and sick, and a number of you have fallen asleep.*

The phrase fallen asleep, or *koimao*, means to die prematurely. In Paul's letter to the Corinthians, when Paul says "for *this* reason," he is referring to "not discerning the Lord's body." The Bible states this is the one and only reason people are not healthy and whole—because of their failure to discern the Lord's Body.

What does the word discern mean? It means to judge correctly, or simply put, to decide between truth and error, or right and wrong. To discern the Body is to know without a doubt that Christ's physical body was beaten for our physical healing. When Jesus broke Bread, He knew that His Body was going to be broken so yours could be made whole.

Think about that for a moment. Did Jesus walk on the water all the time? Did He calm storms all the time? The answer to both of those questions is no. But He healed *all* the time. His nature is to heal. When God brought the children of Israel out of Egypt, He made sure none were sick. Nor did they leave poor. For approximately 2.5 million people to leave Egypt healthy, it had to be a supernatural work of God.

Psalm 105:37 *He brought out Israel, laden with silver and gold, and from among their tribes no one faltered.*

They were prosperous and no one was feeble, weak or sick. That's amazing!

Exodus 15:26 *He said, "If you listen carefully to the Lord your God and do what is right in his eyes, if you pay attention to his commands and keep all his decrees, I will not bring on you any of the diseases I brought on the Egyptians, for I am the Lord, who heals you."*

God hears the prayers of those sick and in bondage and speaks those same words today: *I am the Lord who heals you.*

Malachi 3:6 states, *I the Lord I do not change.* And **Hebrews 13:8** tells us, *Jesus Christ is the same yesterday and today and forever.*

God's will remains the same today even though many have changed God from "I Am" to "I was." He is the same today, yesterday and forever.

Understanding the Bread

Matzo bread is used in today's Jewish Passover celebrations. Matzo bread has slightly burnt holes pricked through the top of the bread with lines running across the surface. One might say the holes represent the piercing of Jesus in His hands, feet and side and the lines represent the stripes on His back and the bruising of His Body.

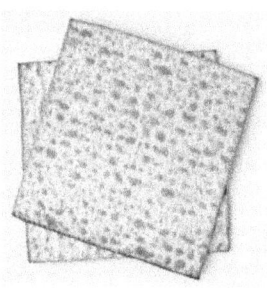

Matzo bread.

Here's another interesting fact. Matzo bread is made without leaven. In Scripture, leaven represents sin, and we know that Jesus had no sin. This feature points directly to sinless Jesus. Matzo bread is a perfect picture of our sinless Savior, complete with wounds and stripes.

Another similarity—bread is made from flour and flour comes from wheat that has been sifted, pounded and beaten over again and again. WHO does that remind you of? It should remind you of Jesus' suffering and sacrifice—for you.

Let's take a closer look at matzo bread used in the Passover Seder.

Bread, unleavened, means without sin (Jesus).

Bread, was pierced with holes (Jesus).

Bread, has stripes or slashes (stripes on Jesus' back).

Bread, at the Passover, the matzo bread is burnt to portray the full fury of God's wrath against our sins (all of which fell upon Jesus).

We know that leaven represents sin in the Bible, but did you know that it also represents erroneous teachings? Leaven is seen as the doctrine of legalism, which condemns people who fail to keep God's laws. Legalism discounts the supernatural and teaches that everything can be explained using reasoning.

Thankfully, Jesus has redeemed us from legalism.

Matthew 16:6 *"Be careful," Jesus said to them. "Be on your guard against the yeast (leaven) of the Pharisees and Sadducees."*

Leviticus 2:11 *Every grain offering you bring to the Lord must be made without yeast, for you are not to burn any yeast or honey in a food offering presented to the Lord.*

Jesus is our grain offering and it must not be mixed with erroneous teaching. The teaching of Jesus unveils the beauty of Christ and the perfection of His finished work on the cross. You have been redeemed from every curse. His sacrifice on the cross was payment for you to enjoy all of God's blessings.

Believe, proclaim and declare that you are healed, not sick. You are prosperous, not poor. You are forever righteous in Christ. Remove any leaven (wrong teaching) from your faith. Allow the anointing of the Holy Spirit to help you confess and believe God's truth, for the Holy Spirit bears witness to the truth.

John 16:13 *But when he, the Spirit of truth, comes, he will guide you into all the truth. He will not speak on his own; he will speak only what he hears, and he will tell you what is yet to come.*

Every day God provided manna for the Israelites while they were traveling in the wilderness. Consider the similarity when we realize Jesus gives us strength through His Word and revelation of Communion. Christ said that He was the Bread come down from heaven and He instructed you to eat His flesh and drink His blood in order to have life.

Understanding the Bread means you've become an enemy of Satan. There is absolutely nothing that the devil fears more than a believer who believes and acts on their revelation concerning the elements of the Lord's Supper. The devil hates Communion, that's for sure.

The Passover Seder Connection

There is a reason communion is closely related to the Passover meal, also called the Passover Seder. When Jews partake of their Passover Seder, they are reminded of their deliverance from 400 years of slavery in Egypt. Communion is a reminder of what Christ has done and how He heals. It is a reminder of the world to come. At the Last Supper, Jesus took the cup and said He would not drink it again until He drank it with His bride (believers) in the kingdom.

Each time Christians eat the Bread and drink the Wine in Communion, they are reminded of their future meal with God, which is referred to in the book of Revelation as the "wedding supper of the Lamb."

Mark 14:25 *"I tell you the truth, I will not drink again from the fruit of the vine until that day when I drink it new in the kingdom of God."*

The apostle Paul tells the believers in Corinth that the Communion supper announces the Lord's death until He comes again. When Jesus returns for the Church and resurrects the dead in Christ, He will take us up to heaven where we will participate in the wedding supper of the Lamb.

Christ will consummate the marriage with His bride with the great banquet supper in heaven.

Revelation 19:7-9 *Let us rejoice and be glad and give him glory! For the wedding of the Lamb has come, and his bride has made herself ready. Fine linen, bright and clean was given her to wear. Then the angel said to me, "Write: 'Blessed are those who are invited to the wedding supper of the Lamb!'" And he added, "These are the true words of God."* (Fine linen stands for the righteous acts of God's holy people.)

1 Thessalonians 4:16-17 *For the Lord himself will come down from heaven, with a loud command, with the voice of the archangel and with the trumpet call of God, and the dead in Christ will rise first. After that, we who are still alive and are left will be caught up together with them in the clouds to meet the Lord in the air. And so we will be with the Lord forever.*

Ephesians 1:9-10 *And he made known to us the mystery of his will according to his good pleasure, which he purposed in Christ to be put into effect when the times will have reached their fulfillment—to bring all things in heaven and on earth together under one head, even Christ.*

This is the time when the dead in Christ will be raised and the living saints will be changed from mortal to immortal. They will be caught up in the clouds to meet the Lord in the air. The apostle Paul called it "being gathered to Him."

2 Thessalonians 2:1 *Concerning the coming of our Lord Jesus Christ and our being gathered to him,....*

At the Marriage Supper of the Lamb, Jesus will once again take the cup, and once and for all, seal the marriage of the bride (believers) and Groom (Jesus)!

Hallelujah, Praise God!

THIS IS MY BODY

> *The more I open my heart to experience the intimate love of my heavenly Father in a deep and personal way, the more I will experience healing, renewal, restoration and transformation in a spectacular way. The more I believe God's grace for me, the more wrong beliefs are uprooted in my life, and the more I shall experience victory supernaturally.*
>
> —Joseph Prince

I don't think the church has a problem with the Blood and forgiveness. In fact, I think we get this. The real question is does the church discern His Body for healing? We have been taught much about the Blood, not so much about the Body. Yet, when we partake of the Lord's Body, there is an infusion of His incorruptible life into your body. Keep in mind that neither sin nor sickness glorifies the Father.

The Bread of Life

Did you know that in Hebrew, Bethlehem, the place of Jesus' birth, means *House of Bread*? How fitting is it that Jesus calls Himself the Bread of life?

Matthew 26:26 *While they were eating, Jesus took bread, and when he had given thanks, he broke it and gave it to his disciples, saying, "Take and eat; this is my body."*

When Jesus said, "Take, eat; this is my body," He was imparting His life, health and wholeness to our bodies. Taking the bread means ingesting His health into our mortal bodies—Jesus imputes His health to us.

Christ, broken on the cross for you, that is the Bread. As you partake of His broken Body, know that His Body was broken so that yours can be whole. Jesus didn't just die for your infirmities and diseases. To be more exact, He took them, or carried them upon Himself. Where did He carry our infirmities and diseases? Think about the three days he went to the lower parts of the earth, in other words, hell. Do you think for one moment He brought sickness back with Him when He was resurrected? I don't think so!

Ephesians 4:8-9 *This is why it says: "When he ascended on high, he led captives in his train and gave gifts to men." (What does "he ascended" mean except that he also descended to the lower, earthly regions?...)*

Faith recognizes and claims the promised benefits that are a result of Christ's body being beaten. In His death, by which all of our physical infirmities, pains, diseases and weaknesses were borne, we are healed. Ask the Holy Spirit to open your eyes to the fact that by His stripes you are healed.

Believe this **TRUTH** and surely your healing will come.

Isaiah 53:4-5 *Surely he took up our infirmities and carried our sorrows, yet we considered him stricken by God, smitten by him, and afflicted. But he was pierced for our transgressions, he was crushed for our iniquities; the* *punishment that brought us peace was upon him, and by his wounds we are healed.*

Twofold Cure

As I've mentioned, the Lord's Supper brings us a twofold cure. Jesus not only took our sins upon Himself, but He also took upon Himself our bodily weaknesses, sicknesses, infirmities and pains. He offers us a replacement for guilt while overcoming the curse of sickness and death—His righteousness and His blessings.

Forgiveness and healing go hand-in-hand. The faith you have for forgiveness is the very same faith that brings healing. Sometimes healing is instant, and sometimes it is gradual. But the more you partake, the better you get. And all of this was provided for in the atonement of Christ. Jesus was the sin offering and the sickness offering. His blood was for forgiveness. Let's not forget that the Blood not only covers our sins but it also satisfies the righteous requirements of God.

Psalm 103:2-3 *Praise the Lord, my soul, and forget not all his benefits—who forgives all your sins and heals all your diseases,...*

If the twofold cure is at work in the Lord's Supper, and it is, you do not have to ask yourself, do I have enough faith? If you do this, you put a hindrance between you and Jesus' finished work. Focus on His finished work and His grace toward you. God sees that as faith.

I like what Joyce Meyers says in her book *Love Out Loud*. She says *to get* is to obtain by effort and struggle but *to receive* is to become a receptacle and simply take in what is being offered.

If the Passover Lamb referred to in Exodus 12 is a foreshadow of Christ, which it was, then like Jesus, the Passover Lamb had to be without blemish or defect. Think about it. If the body and blood of a "shadow lamb" mentioned in the Old Testament could produce the supernatural results we read about in Exodus, how much more can the true Body and Blood of the New Testament lamb bring about?

Luke 22:15-19 *And he said to them, "I have eagerly desired to eat this Passover with you before I suffer. For I tell you, I will not eat it again until it finds fulfillment in the kingdom of God."*
After taking the cup, he gave thanks and said, "Take this and divide it among you. For I tell you I will not drink again from the fruit of the vine until the kingdom of God comes."
And he took bread, gave thanks and broke it, and gave it to them, saying, "This is my body given for you; do this in remembrance of me."

The Passover meal Jesus shares with his disciples is a type, or form of the Lord's Supper. The Blood was for forgiveness and the Bread was for divine strength, or health.

Exodus 12:13 *The blood will be a sign for you on the houses where you are, and when I see the blood, I will pass over you. No destructive plague will touch you when I strike Egypt.*

Luke 22: 20 *In the same way, after the supper he took the cup, saying, "This cup is the new covenant in my blood, which is poured out for you."*

Healing, like forgiveness, is a blood-bought right of Christians. As a Christian, you have a right to walk in divine health. You have a Blood and Body-bought right to God's provision.

Healing is the Children's Bread

When a desperate woman, who is not Jewish, pleads with Jesus to heal her demon-possessed daughter, Jesus spoke to the woman about her daughter's healing. He referred to healing as the "children's bread."

Mark 7:26-28 *The woman was a Greek, born in Syrian Phoenicia. She begged Jesus to drive the demon out of her daughter. "First let the children eat all they want," he told her, "for it is not right to take the children's bread and toss it to the dogs." "Lord," she replied, "even the dogs under the table eat the children's crumbs."*

The word "dogs" referred to the Gentiles. Jesus was saying that healing was only for God's covenant people. At that time, Gentiles were outside the covenant rights of Israel. Yet, when the woman saw the crumbs under the Master's table and voiced her faith, Jesus rewarded her faith.

Faith Rewarded

The woman placed her faith in a little crumb, which released God's healing power to drive the demon out of her daughter.

Mark 7:29 *Then he told her, "For such a reply, you may go; the demon has left your daughter.*

Jesus loved this Gentile woman and her daughter enough to provide the miracle her daughter needed. The woman with the demon-possessed daughter was one of two people the Lord said had great faith. The other person was a centurion, a Roman officer.

Luke 7:1-9 *When Jesus had finished saying all this in the hearing of the people, he entered Capernaum. There a centurion's servant, whom his master valued highly, was sick and about to die. The centurion heard of Jesus and sent some elders of the Jews to him, asking him to come and heal his servant. When they came to Jesus, they pleaded earnestly with him, "This man deserves to have you do this, because he loves our nation and has built our synagogue." So Jesus went with them.*
He was not far from the house when the centurion sent friends to say to him: "Lord, don't trouble yourself, for I do not deserve to have you come under my roof. That is why I did not even consider myself worthy to come to you. But say the word, and my servant will be healed. For I myself am a man under authority, with soldiers under me. I tell this one, 'Go,' and he goes; and that one, 'Come,' and he comes. I say to my servant, 'Do this,' and he does it."
When Jesus heard this, he was amazed at him, and turning to the crowd following him, he said, "I tell you, I have not found such great faith even in Israel."

Jesus rewards faith. Your faith will be rewarded. Praise God!

Jesus, The Healer

Sickness and disease is oppression from the devil and Jesus is our Healer. Let's not forget that Jesus sees healing as the children's bread. Both the woman with the demon-possessed daughter and the centurion were Gentiles, yet they both received healing because of their faith in Jesus.

It's important to know the Old Testament law was added not to bring about redemption but to point out the need for it. When compared to God's holiness, the law made sin even more sinful.

Reflect on this scripture:

Romans 5:19-20 *For just as through the disobedience of the one man the many were made sinners, so also through the obedience of the one man the many will be made righteous. The law was added so that the trespass might increase. But where sin increased, grace increased all the more, so that, just as sin reigned in death, so also grace might reign through righteousness to being eternal life through Jesus Christ our Lord.*

God is willing to extend His grace to you as a believer, His beloved child. Lean on Him and His grace. As His child, you are redeemed and can partake of the Bread from Heaven!

Acts 10:38 *...how God anointed Jesus of Nazareth with the Holy Spirit and power, and how he went around doing good* *and healing all who were under the power of the devil, because God was with him.*

Take a Stand

God has already defeated the devil. He does not need you to do it for Him, nor could you. Jesus defeated the enemy of God and gave *you* the victory. Believers can stand in victory.

Revelation 1:18 *"I am the Living One; I was dead, and behold I am alive for ever and ever! And I hold the keys of death and Hades."*

Ephesians 6:11 *Put on the full armor of God, so that you can take your stand against the devil's schemes.*

The devil wants to make you think that you don't have what you already have. **Stand** means that you don't have to fight— you have already won. The victory is yours!

Resist the temptation to reject what is truth. As I've pointed out, healing was provided for at the cross and is one part of what Communion represents. When the Body for healing is rejected, it is called unbelief. Remember that the broken Bread signifies the stripes that were laid on the back of Jesus releasing you from the curse of sin and death as well as for freedom to enjoy the cure for all manner of diseases. Don't fall into unbelief.

Unbelief can void the promises of God. If you read the promises of healing that comes from the atoning work of Jesus and don't believe it, you won't receive your healing. Do not go through Communion with the attitude of a tester. Do not partake in Communion to see if it works—that is unbelief, not faith.

Please understand that Communion is a vital part of God's covenant with man. His atoning work brought believers into the NEW covenant. Redemption, healing blessings, favor and a home in heaven—all benefits paid in full at Calvary.

You must believe in the healing power of Christ's Body and Blood as well as trust that He is working in your body to bring healing. You cannot trust in any other person or thing. To see healing manifested in your life, you must release your faith and trust in His new covenant. Christ's anointing presence will be there when faith is released.

Hebrews 11:6 *And without faith it is impossible to please God, because anyone who comes to him must believe that he exists and that he rewards those who earnestly seek him.*

The Power of Belief

I heard a pastor share a testimony about a mother of one of his church members who had five surgeries dealing with a cancerous tumor. The surgeon told her son there was a strong likelihood his mother would not pull through. At the time, she was in a coma and on life support.

The son believed so strong in the power of the Lord's Supper that he took a small crumb and a drop of grape juice and placed it in his mother's mouth and declared his mother healed. The pastor reported that the man felt a strong and sweet presence of God in the room when he gave his mother the communion elements.

Three days later, she was conscious and off life support. She went home a week later. This took place in 2011. At the time of this writing, she is healthy and sharing her testimony of what Jesus did for her. So, you see, the Bread, even a small crumb of His Body, is for healing. Because we are God's children we are fully entitled to the healing Bread.

The Bible

Your Bible does you no good unless you use it. When facing the unknown, you can hold it, even kiss it, but until you read and digest it, the Bible will not help you. God's Word does a lot of good when you *receive it as truth* and *speak it as truth*. This is how and when healing comes to deliver you from every evil condition that has been sent to destroy you.

When God wants to heal you, what does He do? He sends His Word. Before God delivers you from your destruction, He sends His Word.

Psalm 107:20 *He sent forth his word and healed them; he rescued them from the grave.*

If you're sick, don't feel condemned. Your Father in heaven loves you and wants you well. But how does your healing come? It comes when you receive His Word on healing that He has already sent you. His promises of healing are all there in your Bible. But you must receive and believe. He meant what He said!

John 5:1-6 *Some time later, Jesus went up to Jerusalem for a feast of the Jews. Now there is in Jerusalem near the Sheep Gate a pool, which in Aramaic is called Bethesda and which is surrounded by five covered colonnades. Here a great number of disabled people used to lie—the blind, the lame, the paralyzed. One who was there had been an invalid for thirty-eight years. When Jesus saw him lying there and learned that he already had been in this condition a long time, He said to him, "Do you want to be made well?"*

Jesus asked the man if he wanted to be well. The question was important because a beggar in those days could lose a sometimes profitable (and easy) income. The man did not see Jesus as His Healer because he was focused on the stirring of the water for healing. Unlike the woman with the issue of blood, Jesus' healing was not limited by this person's misdirected faith.

John 5:6-9 *"Sir," the invalid replied, "I have no man to put me into the pool when the water is stirred. While I am trying to get in, someone else goes down ahead of me.*
Then Jesus said to him, "Get up! Pick up your mat and walk." At once the man was cured; he picked up his mat and walked.

Don't sit around the pool and wait to experience the blessing of healing that Jesus died on the cross to give you. Plead the Body of Jesus and be healed!

The Woman with the Issue of Blood

Jesus was so filled with life that even His clothes were soaked with His health. Remember the woman with the issue of blood for twelve years that came to Jesus knowing that He was her only hope? Just one touch of His garment and she was healed.

Mark 5:25-34 *And a woman was there who had been subject to bleeding for twelve years. She had suffered a great deal under the care of many doctors and had spent all she had, yet instead of getting better she grew worse. When she heard about Jesus, she came up behind him in the crowd and touched his cloak, because she thought, "If I just touch his clothes, I will be healed." Immediately her bleeding stopped and she felt in her body that she was freed from her suffering.*

At once Jesus realized that power had gone out from him. He turned around in the crowd and asked, "Who touched my clothes?"

"You see the people crowding against you," his disciples answered, "and yet you can ask, 'Who touched me?' "

But Jesus kept looking around to see who had done it. Then the woman, knowing what had happened to her, came and fell at his feet and, trembling with fear, told him the whole truth. He said to her, "Daughter, your faith has healed you. Go in peace and be freed from your suffering."

The most important part of this story is that she touched the Healer's cloak because she knew that if she just touched his clothes, she would be healed. This woman believed before she saw the evidence of her healing. She believed in faith and confessed her healing because her confidence was in the Healer, Jesus Christ.

Consider the scripture verse that confirms the woman with an issue of blood's beliefs and actions.

Proverbs 12:18 *The words of the reckless pierce like swords, but the tongue of the wise brings healing.*

The woman with the issue of blood believed in Jesus' goodness and power first then acted in faith, and only then did she feel His healing in her body. She didn't wait until her healing was manifested. Instead, she rejoiced because she knew the Healer.

You can rejoice prior to your manifested healing because Jesus has already borne your diseases and carried your pains. Jesus wants you to know how willing He is to act on your behalf.

Acts 10:34 *Then Peter began to speak: "I now realize how true it is that God does not show favoritism…*

What He did for the woman with the issue of blood, He will do for you. God is not a respecter of persons. The Bible does not say that He healed a few or even many. It says He healed *all* who came to Him in faith, and ALL means all.

Luke 6:19 *…and the people all tried to touch him, because power was coming from him and healing them all.*

Romans 8:32 *He who did not spare his own Son, but gave him up for us all—how will he not also, along with him, graciously give us all things?*

Believing before seeing the evidence of what you believe for is called faith. Faith is like a spark and Jesus is the dynamite power. Did you know that together, you and Jesus, are POWERFUL?

Miraculous Healing

You can experience miraculous healing during Holy Communion, or you can experience miraculous healing gradually. Indeed, the more you partake, the better you will get. Healing is not always instantaneously. It can be a dramatic, in-the-moment, spectacular healing, but if it's not, it is still supernatural and will come with radical results.

Don't be discouraged when you receive 30% of your healing. It just means 70% is on its way. Believe and act on your faith in what God has done for you. Take a stand!

For example, while I was teaching Communion, a woman came to the same class three or four times expecting healing for her shoulder. Her shoulder got better and better each time she participated. Her healing was gradual but definite.

God is pleased when you seek Him expecting to receive by faith. You are the righteousness of God in Christ Jesus. You can't overtake or overdose on God's blessings. You are redeemed! You are blessed!

Maturity in Christ

As believers, we need to progress in our maturity and move beyond the elementary teaching we have received. The mature Body of Christ should operate just as Jesus did over two thousand years ago. In fact, Jesus says we will do greater works than He did. We need to be that divine, fully mature, anointed Body of believers. Our priority should be to grow deep and reach wide.

John 14:12 *I tell you the truth, anyone who has faith in me will do what I have been doing.*

1 Corinthians 3:2 *I gave you milk, not solid food, for you were not yet ready for it. Indeed, you are still not ready.*

Hebrews 5:12 *In fact, though by this time you ought to be teachers, you need someone to teach you the elementary truths of God's word all over again. You need milk, not solid food!*

For way too long, Christians have been made to be fearful and **SIN** conscious. God wants you to be **SON** conscious. He wants you to place your faith in His Son's work and nothing else. When you celebrate Communion you should remember the resurrection as well as the death of Christ.

The curse under the Old Testament law is no longer in effect. Believers have entered into the blessing of Grace under the New Covenant established by the Blood and Body of Christ. Believers no longer live according to the law given at Mt. Sinai. Believers now live at Mt. Zion, where Jesus' Body and Blood were shed for the sins of mankind.

> Because of Jesus, we went from
>
> **OLD TESTAMENT Mt. Sinai**...
>
> ...to **NEW TESTAMENT Mt. Zion**.
>
> Because of the cross, we go from
>
> **SIN consciousness**...
>
> ...to **SON consciousness**

We are redeemed from the curse of the law of sin and death. We are victorious because of His love, grace and mercy.

The Most Significant Story Ever Told

The most significant story ever told begins with Adam eating the forbidden fruit. This is what plunged us into sin consciousness, bringing with it disease and untimely death. But the story ends with us accepting God's grace and consuming the Bread (or His Body), which brings health, and drinking the Wine (or His Blood) for wholeness.

Also, if Jesus has taken your sickness, He cannot "untake" it. You may find it hard to believe, but the *truth* is still the **truth**. Everything was paid for because God said it is a *finished* work. My hope for everyone reading this is that when you approach His Table, your faith would be stirred up and you would experience His presence and love for you afresh. Now declare and proclaim by faith what Jesus did for you!

1 Corinthians 11:23-26 *For I received from the Lord what I also passed on to you: the Lord Jesus, on the night he was betrayed, took bread, and when he had given thanks, he broke it and said, "This is my body, which is for you; do this in remembrance of me." In the same way, after supper he took the cup, saying, "This cup is the new covenant in my blood; do this, whenever you drink it, in remembrance of me." For whenever you eat this bread and drink this cup, you proclaim the Lord's death until he comes.*

Hear Him saying, "Take, eat. This is My Body, which is broken for you." See His eyes burning with love as He says to you, "This cup is the new covenant in My Blood, which is shed for you. See Jesus carrying all your physical conditions, pains, diseases, and hurts on His Body. Visualize that condition on His Body. It is no longer on you. See His health and wholeness come on you. He carried them for you. Release your faith in the Bread and the Wine.

God is not saying that your sickness does not exist, nor is He asking you to pretend that it is not there. He is asking you to look away from the sickness, painful as it may be, and look to the Truth. Sickness has already been judged at the cross in the Body of His Son.

Use Words Wisely

God's way of faith is to call those things that are not as though they are. And because you are made in God's image, you can also call those things that are not as though they are.

Proverbs 12:18 *Reckless words pierce like a sword, but the tongue of the wise brings healing.*

Romans 4:17 *As it is written: "I have made you a father of many nations." He is our father in the sight of God, in whom he believed—the God who gives life to the dead and calls things that are not as though they were.*

For example, when Jesus saw the man with a shriveled hand, He said, "Stretch out your hand!" He called forth what He wanted.

Matthew 12:13 *Then he said to the man, "Stretch out your hand." So he stretched it out and it was completely restored, just as sound as the other.*

Jesus looked at the paralytic and called forth his healing. Jesus saw the man the way God intended him to be, and He called it forth.

Matthew 9:6 *"But so that you may know that the Son of Man has authority on earth to forgive sins…" Then he said to the paralytic, "Get up, take your mat and go home."*

You can call forth your healing even if you don't feel healed. Change the way you speak and start calling forth your healing and wholeness the way God meant for it to be. Jesus is the Word, the very Bread of Life to heal. Just as God ascribes His righteousness to you, He also imputes His healing to you.

Abundant life means life to the fullest today. Abundant life goes way beyond material things. Abundant living is the supernatural plan of God.

John 10:10 *The thief comes only to steal and kill and destroy; I have come that they may have life, and have it to the full.*

If the Blood of Jesus saved you, then the power of Jesus raises and empowers you and the Body of Jesus heals you. Proclaim, affirm and declare these facts. Tell your body to line up with what Scripture says, and surely, you will find that you are healed. Don't be robbed of this tremendous blessing.

Come boldly to the Lord's Table and receive afresh His health, His wholeness and His life. Come to His Table and receive all that He has for you.

THIS IS MY BLOOD

When God looks at me today, He sees me in Christ. He does not see my imperfections, but sees His Son's Blood, and therefore accepts me completely and loves me unconditionally.

—Joseph Prince

In the Old Testament, under the law, God required the blood sacrifice of animals for the atonement of sins because His people were unfaithful. The Israelites sought after other gods, which displeased God.

Leviticus 17:11 *For the life of a creature is in the blood, and I have given it to you to make atonement for yourselves on the altar; it is the blood that makes atonement for one's life.*

Leviticus 4:3-5 *If the anointed priest sins, bringing guilt on the people, he must bring to the LORD a young bull without defect as a sin offering for the sin he has committed. He is to present the bull at the entrance to the Tent of Meeting before the LORD. He is to lay his hand on its head and slaughter it there before the LORD. Then the anointed priest shall take some of the bull's blood and carry it into the Tent of Meeting.*

Ultimately, a better sacrifice was needed. The blood of animals would not suffice.

Hebrews 10:4 *But those sacrifices are an annual reminder of sins, because it is impossible for the blood of bulls and goats to take away sins.*

The New Covenant

About six hundred years before Christ's coming, God promised His people, the Jews, that He would establish a new covenant. You will see that this covenant would also require blood.

Jeremiah 31:31-34 *"The time is coming," declares the LORD, "when I will make a new covenant with the people of Israel and with the people of Judah. It will not be like the covenant I made with their forefathers when I took them by the hand to lead them out of Egypt, because they broke my covenant, though I was a husband to them," declares the LORD.*
"This is the covenant I will make with the House of Israel after that time," declares the LORD. "I will put my law in their minds and write it on their hearts. I will be their God, and they will be my people. No longer will a man teach his neighbor, or a man his brother, saying, 'Know the LORD,' because they will all know me, from the least of them to the greatest," declares the LORD. "For I will forgive their wickedness and will remember their sins no more."

So you see, we have two covenants in the Bible; one is found in the Old Testament, and the other in the New Testament. Both were entered and ushered into by blood. The Old Testament covenant came by the blood of animals and the New Testament covenant came by the blood of Jesus Christ.

Old Testament:
Exodus 24:8 *Moses then took the blood, sprinkled it on the people and said, "This is the blood of the covenant that the LORD has made with you in accordance with all these words."*

New Testament:
Hebrews 9:18-22 *This is why even the first covenant was not put into effect without blood. When Moses had proclaimed every commandment of the law to all the people, he took the blood of calves, together with water, scarlet wool and branches of hyssop, and sprinkled the scroll and all the people. He said, "This is the blood of the covenant, which God has commanded you to keep." In the same way, he sprinkled with the blood both the tabernacle and everything used in its ceremonies. In fact, the law requires that nearly everything be cleansed with blood, and without the shedding of blood there is no forgiveness.*

Matthew 26:28 *This is my blood of the covenant, which is poured out for many for the forgiveness of sins.*

The Final Sacrifice

The animal sacrifices of the Old Testament were a depiction of the final sacrifice. When Jesus Christ went to the cross over two thousand years ago, He became the ultimate and final sacrifice.

Consider the following:

His skin was whipped off. **(Psalm 22:17)**

His beard was torn out of his cheeks. **(Isaiah 50:6)**

*They spit in His face. **(Matthew 26:67)***

*His head pierced with thorns. **(Mark 15:17)***

*His face beaten to a pulp. He was unrecognizable. The Bible says that Jesus' face was more marred than any man. **(Matthew 26:67; Isaiah 52:14; Mark 14:65)***

*His hands and feet were nailed all the way through with spikes. **(John 20:25; Colossians 2:14)***

*His side pierced with a spear after He died. **(John 19:34)***

The sacrifice of Jesus Christ, the Son of God, completely abolished the system of animal sacrifice forever. Animal sacrifices in the Old Testament is a foreshadow of the true sacrifice of Jesus Christ. Animal blood prefigured the true blood that would be shed thousands of years later on a cross outside the city of Jerusalem.

Hebrews 9: 11-14 *When Christ came as high priest of the good things that are now already here, he went through the greater and more perfect tabernacle that is not man-made, that is to say, is not a part of this creation. He did not enter by means of the blood of goats and calves; but he entered the Most Holy Place once for all by his own blood, thus obtaining eternal redemption. The blood of goats and bulls and the ashes of a heifer sprinkled on those who are ceremonially unclean sanctify them so that they are outwardly clean. How much more, then, will the blood of Christ, who through the eternal Spirit offered himself unblemished to God, cleanse our consciences from acts that lead to death, so that we may serve the living God!*

Jesus offered himself a sacrifice once, and for all. He was offered Himself to be the final sacrifice so that He could bear the sins of many.

Hebrews 7:27 *Unlike the other high priests, he does not need to offer sacrifices day after day, first for his own sins, and then for the sins of the people. He sacrificed for their sins once for all when he offered himself.*

Hebrews 9:28 *...so Christ was sacrificed once to take away the sins of many; and he will appear a second time, not to bear sin, but to bring salvation to those who are waiting for him.*

Hebrews 10:10 *And by that will, we have been made holy through the sacrifice of the body of Jesus Christ once for all.*

The Blood of Jesus is powerful. Consider what the Blood of Jesus has done for you.

Jesus is Your Shield

The Romans made battle shields using leather animal skins. In order to provide the necessary protection, they used seven layers of skin to make it four or five inches thick and then nailed everything to a wooden framework. A single layer was not sufficient for the shield to be effective.

In preparation for battle, Roman soldiers dipped their shields into water, saturating them in order to stop and quench flaming arrows. This was because one of the most advanced weapons at the time was the flaming arrow. It contained a ball of linen dipped in tar. The intention was to ignite the linen under the opposing soldier's breastplate and thereby consume him. The multi-layered shield created a wall to protect the Roman soldier from flaming arrows.

The equivalent for the Christian soldier is referred to as the shield of faith, spoken of in the New Testament.

Ephesians 6:16 *In addition to all this, take up the shield of faith, with which you can extinguish all the flaming arrows of the evil one.*

In Old Testament times, the Romans used seven layers of animal skins to create defensive battle shields. In the New Testament, God provided an even more perfect shield. Jesus came to be your shield. He was stretched out and nailed to a wooden framework, the cross. Just like a shield, His purpose was to receive upon Himself all the afflictions Satan intended for you. He came to take upon Himself every arrow that Satan intended for you.

God wants you to know that He has given you a shield and His name is Jesus! He has provided a shield that will protect you from whatever the enemy brings against you. The shield is your defense and your protection. The shield of faith blocks and guards you against an enemy's attack just like the Romans used their shield for protection in warfare.

It is important to realize that Satan will shoot his fiery darts once a person starts to stand on and trust in the Word of God. Attacks may intensify the more we do for Christ.

2 Timothy 3:12 *In fact, everyone who wants to live a godly life in Christ Jesus will be persecuted, ...*

However, victory over all the attacks of the enemy is possible. The Apostle Paul said, "Now thanks be unto God, which always causes us to triumph in Christ." Paul had great opposition, but he was always victorious in the end.

Sadly, complete and total victory is not common among Christians. And from the viewpoint of some, it may be nonexistent, but that is not because it is not available. Bible teacher Andrew Womack said, "Teaching that God wills us to fail at times is like telling athletes that their coach wants them to lose."

We all learn from defeats, and losing can be used to make us better people, but winners never plan to lose. Your shield has a name. It's JESUS!

The Veil is Gone, the Curtain is Open

In the Old Testament, God's dwelling place on earth was called the Tabernacle. This is where the Ark of the Covenant, containing the Ten Commandments, was kept. It was a sacred place, to be sure, which is why a veil, or a curtain, separated the Most Holy Place from the Holy Place inside the Tabernacle of God.

Exodus 26: 33 *Hang the curtain from the clasps and place the ark of the Testimony behind the curtain. The curtain will separate the Holy Place from the Most Holy Place.*

In the New Testament, the Body of Jesus, the ultimate sacrifice, opened the curtain to God Almighty. He tore the veil and made a way to God. No longer is there a veil to separate or conceal us from the Most Holy Place. We enter the Holy of Holies by the Blood of Jesus.

Hebrews 10:19-22 *Therefore, brothers, since we have confidence to enter the Most Holy Place by the blood of Jesus, by a new and living way opened for us through the curtain, that is, his body, and since we have a great priest over the house of God, let us draw near to God with a sincere heart in full assurance of faith, having our hearts sprinkled to cleanse us from a guilty conscience and having our bodies washed with pure water.*

Under the old covenant, the high priest carried the blood of animals into the Most Holy Place as a sin offering. However, the bodies had to be burned outside the city gate.

Hebrews 13:11-12 *The high priest carries the blood of animals into the Most Holy Place as a sin offering, but the bodies are burned outside the camp. And so Jesus also suffered outside the city gate to make the people holy through his own blood.*

Did you notice that the body of the sin offering was taken outside the city to be burned? In the same manner, Jesus didn't die in the city of Jerusalem. Jesus' Body suffered outside the city of Jerusalem, in Golgotha. The point is that the veil is gone and a curtain will never again separate God from the sins of man.

2 Corinthians 3:16 *But whenever anyone turns to the Lord, the veil is taken away.*

Life in the Blood

There is life in the Blood and the Body of Christ. Do you know this? Perhaps you do not realize just how much the Blood and Body of the Master affects and changes mankind. There is power in the Body and the Blood found at His Communion Table. You must declare it and accept no counterfeits.

Forgiveness, the Healing Balm

One of the great comforts afforded to us by the Holy Spirit is forgiveness. It allows us to go on with our lives. When we forgive, the link between our past and us is broken. Sadly, many times the person hardest to forgive is the one in the mirror. There is no healing medicine, or balm, for pain as powerful as forgiveness. There is no healing in blame, whether it is yourself or someone else. Forgiveness is so valuable you can't put a price on it.

Jeremiah 8:22 *Is there no balm in Gilead? Is there no physician there? Why then is there no healing for the wound of my people?*

God wants to bless you *and* answer your prayers. That is why He tells you to deal with your sins. Once you understand and accept Christ's sacrifice for your sins and repent from wrongdoing, you can (and should) clean out any secret closets of sin and disobedience. This is what brings comfort to us and heals us.

1 John 1:9 *If we confess our sins, he is faithful and just and will forgive us our sins and purify us from all unrighteousness.*

The One Thing

If we do one thing, confess our sins, God will do four things. He will:

Be faithful.

Be just.

Forgive our sins.

Cleanse us from all unrighteousness.

Romans 3:22-23 *This righteousness from God comes through faith in Jesus Christ to all who believe. There is no difference, for all have sinned and fall short of the glory of God,...*

1 John 1:7-8 *But if we walk in the light, as he is in the light, we have fellowship with one another, and the blood of Jesus, his Son, purifies us from all sin. If we claim to be without sin, we deceive ourselves and the truth is not in us.*

Be truthful about your transgressions against God. Agree with Him about what He calls sin. You can't surprise God or shock Him. He is shock proof. He already knows everything. In ancient times, it was often assumed that a calamity would only befall those who were extremely sinful. But Jesus pointed out that all are sinners. Everyone must repent.

Luke 13:1-5 *Now there were some present at that time who told Jesus about the Galileans whose blood Pilate had mixed with their sacrifices. Jesus answered, "Do you think that these Galileans were worse sinners than all the other Galileans because they suffered this way? I tell you, no! But unless you repent, you too will all perish. Or those eighteen who died when the tower in Siloam fell on them—do you think they were more guilty than all the others living in Jerusalem? I tell you, no! But unless you repent, you too will all perish."*

1 John 1:10 *If we claim we have not sinned, we make him out to be a liar and his word is not in us.*

This truth was written to Christian believers who already had a relationship with Christ. The point is not to go around feeling guilty about sins, but rather to ask for forgiveness and be cleansed. Be cleansed continually so that you can live before God in holiness. God is essentially saying to you if you want me to do business with you, you have to get rid of sin, disobedience, and neglect. God is gracious, but your iniquities have separated you from God; your sins have hidden His face from you.

Isaiah 59:2 *But your iniquities have separated you from your God; your sins have hidden his face from you, so that he will not hear.*

You can ask God to forgive you for sins you don't realize you're committing. King David prayed to be forgiven of his hidden faults.

Psalm 19:12-13 *But who can discern his errors? Forgive my hidden faults. Keep your servant also from willful sins; may* *they not rule over me. Then I will be blameless, innocent of great transgression.*

King David desired five things:

Cleanse me from secret faults.

Keep me from presumptuous sins.

Let no sin dominate.

Let my words be acceptable to God.

Let the meditation of my heart be acceptable to God.

What a prayer!

We also have this promise from God's Word.

Psalm 103:11-12 *For as high as the heavens are above the earth, so great is his love for those who fear him; as far as the east is from the west, so far has he removed our transgressions from us.*

This is equivalent to blotting out our sin.

Acts 3:19 *Repent, then, and turn to God, so that your sins may be wiped out, that times of refreshing may come from the Lord,...*

Some definitions:

Repent—to change your mind for better, morally speaking; change your attitude toward sin. When convinced that Jesus is the Messiah, you change your mind and let your heart be contrite for sins you've committed against Him.

Matthew 3:2; 4:17; Acts 2:38; 3:19; Luke 13:1-5

Be converted—your conduct changes; you turned around, headed in a new direction; you begin a new walk with God that is destined to become a blessed journey.

Psalm 19:7; 51:13; Matthew 18:3; James 5:19

Isaiah 43:25 *"I, even I, am he who blots out your transgressions, for my own sake, and remembers your sins no more.*

The idea of blotting out sins is taken from the custom of keeping accounts and blotting out the charge when the debt is paid. God promises to cancel your sin when you confess and repent. No payment can be exacted for the sins Jesus has paid the debt for—you are forgiven and completely pardoned.

As a sinner, you do not deserve forgiveness. You deserve full punishment but God grants you free grace and the full pardon of all sin along with the cancellation of punishment for rebellion. Besides Him, there is no Savior. Jesus is the reason you escape hell. You owe your life to Him. Live for His glory!

Isaiah 44:22 *"I have swept away your offenses like a cloud, your sins like the morning mist. Return to me, for I have redeemed you."*

Your Full Potential is in God

You are either becoming the person you want to be, or you're becoming the person God wants you to be. Desire to be the person God wants you to be and created you to be. Yearn to live with the full potential He has placed inside of you. Don't let rejection or hurts take this away. Those who hurt you don't get to decide who you are going to be.

Keep in mind, the hands that hurt you are not nearly as big as the hands that protect and love you. God's promises are bigger than any problem you might have. Knowing that God's promises are bigger than your problems will change your view of any crises you might have to face in the future.

There is no unity without forgiveness. Your willingness to forgive others allows you to be blessed now and in the future. Will you allow God's grace and the promises of heaven to help you live in unity with others today? No other word sums up the character of Christ in relationship to us like the word forgiveness.

We never look more like Christ than when we forgive.

1 Peter 3:8-9 *Finally, all of you, live in harmony with one another; be sympathetic, love as brothers, be compassionate and humble. Do not repay evil with evil or insult with insult, but with blessing, because to this you were called so that you may inherit a blessing.*

I can promise you that there will be times when you will not feel like granting forgiveness. When I first began to pray the prayer of forgiveness, I am certain that my heart did not line up with my confession. Yet I knew I could not let my feelings be in charge. Eventually, while exercising obedience, my heart caught up with my words. I chose to believe, proclaim and act upon God's word.

Someone gave me some good advice. They said that if you desire God's fire to burn brightly in your heart, you must take out yesterday's ashes. I took that to mean that if I wanted to experience God's abundant plan for my life, I had to get rid of yesterday's sins and any leftover unforgiveness.

Remember, you are never more like God than when you choose to forgive. And when you don't forgive, it is as if you are telling God that you don't trust Him to handle the situation. Trust God.

The Benefits of Forgiveness

We can receive the Bread of Communion daily; however, we must also feed from the Scriptures and every word that comes from God. If you receive the Bread of Communion, yet in your heart you despise your brother, you are breaking the New Covenant commandment to love and forgive your enemies.

Luke 4:4 *Jesus answered, "It is written: 'Man shall not live on bread alone.'"*

Matthew 5:44 *But I tell you: love your enemies and pray for those who persecute you.*

When you are claiming healing for yourself, if you have not forgiven those who have wronged you, you must first forgive them of their trespasses. You cannot hold them or their trespasses hostage in your heart. Can we expect the healing power of God to work in our lives if we are eating the Bread and not walking in obedience to the Word of God?

This is why we are told to confess our faults to one another and pray for each other so that we may be healed.

Matthew 6:14-15 *For if you forgive men when they sin against you, your heavenly Father will also forgive you. But if you do not forgive men their sins, your Father will not forgive your sins.*

Matthew 18:34-35 *"In anger his master turned him over to the jailers to be tortured, until he should pay back all he owed. This is how my heavenly Father will treat each of you unless you forgive your brother from your heart."*

Living with unforgiveness is a steep price to pay. Unforgiveness breeds negative feelings where a root of bitterness can develop and grow. Don't give the enemy an open door. Don't let Satan capture a part of your heart that you really do not want him to have. According to Scripture, prayers can be hindered, and in some cases, prayers can go unheard.

1 Peter 3:7 *Husbands, in the same way be considerate as you live with your wives, and treat them with respect as the* *weaker partner and as heirs with you of the gracious gift of life, so that nothing will hinder your prayers.*

Christ often spoke of forgiveness and healing together when He healed the sick.

James 5: 14-16 *Is any one of you sick? He should call the elders of the church to pray over them and anoint him with oil in the name of the Lord. And the prayer offered in faith will make the sick person well; the Lord will raise him up. If he has sinned, he will be forgiven. Therefore confess your sins to each other and pray for each other so that you may be healed. The prayer of a righteous person is powerful and effective.*

John 5:14-15 *Later Jesus found him at the temple and said to him, "See, you are well again. Stop sinning or something worse may happen to you." The man went away and told the Jewish leaders that it was Jesus who had made him well.*

Matthew 9:2-7 *Some men brought to him a paralytic, lying on a mat. When Jesus saw their faith, he said to the man, "Take heart, son; your sins are forgiven."*
At this, some of the teachers of the law said to themselves, "This fellow is blaspheming!"
Knowing their thoughts, Jesus said, "Why do you entertain evil thoughts in your hearts? Which is easier: to say, 'Your sins are forgiven,' or to say, 'Get up and walk'? But so that you may know that the Son of Man has authority on earth to forgive sins..." Then he said to the paralytic, "Get up, take your mat and go home." Then the man got up and went home.

Forgiveness is a Choice

It is a willful choice you make to forgive others just as Christ forgave you. How much more should we forgive others when we have been forgiven so much? Jesus' model prayer stresses this fact so well.

Matthew 6:9-13 *"This, then, is how you should pray:*
'Our Father in heaven, hallowed be your name, your kingdom come, your will be done, on earth as it is in heaven. Give us today our daily bread. Forgive us our debts, as we also have forgiven our debtors. And lead us not into temptation, but deliver us from the evil one.'

Forgiveness is necessary prior to enjoying spiritual and emotional well-being. Before asking for, or receiving healing, we must examine our motives and relationship with both God and our fellow man.

Holding onto offenses can make you physically ill. Did you know that the benefits of forgiveness have been medically and scientifically proven? It may come as a surprise to find out that forgiving is a skill you can own and that granting forgiveness may actually do more for you than the person you forgive.

Harvard Women's Health Watch discussed five positive health effects stemming from the act of forgiving.

They are:

Reduced Stress

Researchers found that mentally nursing a grudge puts your body through the same strains as a major stressful event. Muscles tense, blood pressure rises, and sweating increases.

Better Heart Health

One study found a link between forgiving someone for a betrayal and improvements in blood pressure and heart rate, indicating a decreased workload for the heart.

Stronger Relationships

A study showed that women who were able to forgive their spouses and feel benevolent toward them resolved conflicts more effectively.

Reduced Pain

A study on people with chronic back pain found that those who practiced meditation, focusing on converting anger to compassion, felt less pain and anxiety than those who received regular care.

Greater Happiness

When you forgive someone, you make yourself—rather than the person who hurt you—responsible for your happiness. One survey showed that people who talked about forgiveness during psychotherapy sessions experience greater improvements than those who didn't.

Do not allow unforgiveness to control you or hinder your spiritual blessings. When you hold onto offenses you stop the healing power of God from flowing. Get rid of unforgiveness as soon as you recognize it. Holding onto grudges does not please God. Remember, unforgiveness is an unnecessary and easily removable roadblock on your way to experiencing healing.

Confidence in Prayer

Confidence is essential when it comes to strengthening your spirit and prayer life. Guilt is associated with condemnation, but freedom from condemnation produces confidence when we pray.

We may abandon God, but God never abandons us. In Psalm 10, David writes how he thought God was hiding somewhere, unavailable to solve his problems.

Psalm 10:1 *Why, O LORD, do you stand far off? Why do you hide yourself in times of trouble?*

We must trust God completely even when God seems unreachable or hidden. During the dark times of life, we must continue to love Him. Remember, we are the ones who stand in the way of God working on our behalf. God never abandons us.

Consider the story of Joseph and his brothers. Like Joseph, has someone sold you out? Are you trying to punish them for what they've done? Have you thought about how trusting God's purpose for your life can help you get beyond your need to get even? Which do you see more clearly—the pain of the past, or God at work in your life? Do you believe that when you have unforgiveness in your heart that it blocks your spirit from receiving revelation knowledge from the Lord?

On the other hand, problems may be happening to you because the devil is attacking your faith. That means you are a threat to Satan. And yes, you are in a war with him. But guess what? We know the end of the story and we win. Praise God!

Calvary represents the kingdom of God and all the benefits that Jesus paid for by suffering and dying on the cross. These include:

Forgiveness.

Healing.

Prosperity.

Victory over sin and the devil.

Let's not forget that Christ did not die on the cross until He prayed, "Father, forgive them, for they know not what they do." Jesus knew that He could not die and redeem mankind from sin if He, Himself, died with unforgiveness toward those who had crucified Him.

Stephen, one of Christ's disciples, asked God not to hold the sin of his death against those who murdered him—even as he was being stoned!

Acts 7:60 *Then he fell on his knees and cried out, "Lord, do not hold this sin against them." When he had said this, he fell asleep.*

Both of those prayers had amazing results.

Power of Proclaiming

When you participate in Holy Communion, you are proclaiming to demon spirits that they have been disarmed and Jesus reigns supreme. When you release your faith in the complete and perfect work of Jesus at the cross, you are releasing the power of the Holy Communion, which proclaims the Lord's death.

1 Corinthians 11: 26 *For whenever you eat this bread and drink this cup, you proclaim the Lord's death until he comes.*

Every knee must bow and every tongue confesses that Jesus Christ is Lord.

Philippians 2: 9-11 *Therefore God exalted him to the highest place and gave him the name that is above every name, that at the name of Jesus every knee should bow, in heaven and on earth and under the earth, and every tongue confess that Jesus Christ is Lord, to the glory of God the Father.*

Thank you, Daddy God!

TAKING COMMUNION

If angels could be jealous of men, they would be so for one reason: Holy Communion.

—Maximilian Kolbe

Anywhere, Anytime

Did you know that you can take Communion anywhere, at anytime? Location is not important as long as you're able to keep your focus on Him. Spending a few moments of quality time with the Lord is not difficult. I've taken Communion in restaurants and other various places. Even though these places may not have been ideal, I was still able to tune out the distractions around me. I needed to be intimate with my Jesus and I wanted to take Communion—where I was at the time did not matter.

Remember, taking Communion is not a ritual. It is a precious sacred moment between you and the Lord. God will not ignore your worship of Him when it is done sincerely. It doesn't matter where you are when you do it, and it doesn't matter if you use grape juice, water, cracker or bread. God is compassionate and moved by what's in your heart.

Communion should be observed whether you are sick or healthy. It can be done daily, weekly or whenever with a spirit of understanding and faith. Communion at our home can be a part of our intimate time with Jesus. The key is to believe that as you receive the very life of Christ, He is working in your body, driving out every sickness, disease and weakness that is trying to hinder your quality of life.

I don't think you can receive Communion too often. Partaking in The Lord's Supper often doesn't mean it will lose its meaning or become too familiar. Likewise, I don't believe you can read the Bible too often or get tired of His Word. You cannot pray too often and lose the importance of prayer. Never fear that spending a lot of time with the Lord will somehow become something dull and ordinary. Being intimate with Jesus is extraordinary and always supernatural.

As you spend time with the Lord, keep in mind that every promise in the New Covenant is released through faith. The promises found in the Word of God must be mixed with faith. The Bible tells us Christ could not do miracles because of unbelief.

Matthew 13:58 *And he did not do many miracles there because of their lack of faith.*

Have faith. You can trust God's Word.

Is it Just a Piece of Bread?

The manner in which you partake will determine whether you experience the benefits of the Lord's Body. If your attitude is that it's just a piece of bread, then that is what it will be. And you will have robbed yourself of the life-giving effects of the Bread at His Table.

The Greek word for unworthy used in 1 Corinthians 11:27 is *anaxios*. By eating the bread or drinking the cup in an unworthy manner we sin against the Body and Blood of the Lord. With regard to the Lord's Supper, the Apostle Paul corrected believers in Corinth by urging them to partake in the correct manner.

1 Corinthians 11:27 *So then, whoever eats the bread or drinks the cup of the Lord in an unworthy manner will be guilty of sinning against the body and blood of the Lord.*

Some believers in Corinth did not approach the Lord's Supper with the right attitude. We are not to treat the Lord's Supper as a common meal. We should not consider the bread and the cup as common things. We are to acknowledge the solemn impartation.

1 Corinthians 11:20-22 *When you come together, it is not the Lord's Supper you eat, for as you eat, each of you goes ahead without waiting for anybody else. One remains hungry, another gets drunk. Don't you have homes to eat and drink in? Or do you despise the church of God and humiliate those who have nothing? What shall I say to you? Shall I praise you for this? Certainly not!*

Have you always taken Communion correctly? Probably not. I know that I haven't and I had to repent. However, when we continue in His Word, He is faithful to grant us more and more revelation of exactly what He is teaching us.

Jesus wants you to take the Bread and believe that His Body was broken so that your body can be made well. And when you discern it that way, you are partaking in a worthy manner. When you come to His Table, release your faith in the healing found and released in the Lord's Body. It is not a question of whether it is God's will to heal you. It is only a question of when God will heal you.

Order

In the church, there must be order, and so clergy, elders or those who have been given authority to administer Holy Communion have served the Lord's Supper. But once you have become a believer in Christ and understand the power of His resurrection, you have become a priest and a minister unto the Lord, which means you can partake of the Lord's Supper any time, as often as you like. You do not need clergy to serve Communion. You, too, can serve Communion to others.

1 Peter 2:9 *But you are a chosen people, a royal priesthood, a holy nation, a people belonging to God, that you may declare the praises of him who called you out of darkness into his wonderful light.*

Believers are called a kingdom of priests and a holy nation. Unfortunately, religious traditions keep believers from acting as priests unto God as intended in the New Testament. We respect and honor leadership when they serve the elements, but Paul did not list it as one of the duties of a bishop.

1 Timothy 3:1-7 *Here is a trustworthy saying: If anyone sets his heart on being an overseer, he desires a noble task. Now* *the overseer must be above reproach, the husband of but one wife, temperate, self-controlled, respectable, hospitable, able to teach, not given to drunkenness, not violent but gentle, not quarrelsome, not a lover of money. He must manage his own family well and see that his children obey him with proper respect. (If anyone does not know how to manage his own family, how can he take care of God's church?) He must not be a recent convert, or he may become conceited and fall under the same judgment as the devil. He must also have a good reputation with outsiders, so that he will not fall into disgrace and into the devil's trap.*

In the early church, believers traveled from house to house, serving Communion daily. The breaking of Bread was a consistent, daily practice among believers in the early church.

Acts 2:46 *Every day they continued to meet together in the temple courts. They broke bread in their homes and ate together with glad and sincere hearts, praising God and enjoying the favor of all the people.*

Holy Communion is a mindset and a heart-felt act. God knows your heart. When done with the right heart and motive, what you're doing becomes holy, just as He is holy. Keep in mind that because we can boldly approach our Daddy God with all of our needs and desires, we do not need a mortal man to confess or intercede on our behalf before God almighty. And we do not need wine or bread to partake. I've used water and a cookie although I keep grape juice and bread in my refrigerator so I can partake often.

Taking Communion in an Unworthy Manner

Have you asked yourself what does it mean to partake in an unworthy manner?

This revelation set me free. Partaking in an unworthy manner means not recognizing that the broken Body of the Lord was meant to bring health and wholeness. If you fail to discern or understand the significance of the Lord's Body, you are eating and drinking in an unworthy manner. You make what Jesus did on the cross of no effect for you.

1 Corinthians 11:27-30 *Therefore, whoever eats the bread or drink the cup of the Lord in an unworthy manner will be guilty of sinning against the body and blood of the Lord. A man ought to examine himself before he eats of the bread and drinks of the cup. For anyone who eats and drinks without recognizing the body of the Lord eats and drinks judgment on himself. That is why many among you are weak and sick, and a number of you have fallen asleep (died).*

The devil has tried to make the church (believers) feel unworthy or unfit to come to the Lord's Table. In doing so, he has stolen powerful truths established at the Lord's Table. As long as the church continues to have a wrong perception of God, the devil can talk believers into a life of defeat.

Consider this:

The Old Testament covenant demanded righteousness; the law was dependent upon man and his obedience.

But the New Testament covenant provided righteousness; God's grace is dependent upon Jesus and His obedience.

Him Alone

It's DONE, and it is not about our perfection. It's about the Perfect One, Jesus Christ!

The more revelation you receive of His finished work, the more you will receive an impartation of faith for any situation, even the seemingly impossible ones!

I want to be clear. There is no power in the elements, the Bread or the Wine. The power is in the faith that the elements are what Jesus said they are. It is not the sacrament that saves you or heals you. It is all about Jesus and your obedience.

Philippians 4:6 *Do not be anxious about anything, but in everything, by prayer and petition, with thanksgiving, present your requests to God.*

My daddy use to say, "Heaven's kill for earthly ills" but until I did this study, I did not know what he was talking about. Jesus was Heaven's kill for all *my* earthly ills! Jesus took my place so that I might take His place. Praise God!

Jesus didn't deserve to be made sin and you don't deserve His righteousness, but that's the Gospel message. That is the Good News and what is commonly called the Divine Exchange.

You don't deserve healing but by His stripes you are healed, not because of your works, but because of His FINISHED WORK! You can't add to God's work. It is Jesus Christ ALONE, never Jesus plus your efforts, your understanding, or even your faithfulness. It's HIM, and HIM ALONE! Not partly on Him and partly on you.

IT IS ALL HIM!!!

What Does it Mean to Drink Judgment?

Perhaps you have stumbled around this verse:

1 Corinthians 11:29 *For those who eat and drink without discerning the body of Christ eat and drink judgment on themselves.*

The judgment in this verse does not mean God's anger or wrath. Judgment in this case means *divine sentence*. When Adam sinned against God, a divine sentence fell on the human race. Weakness, sickness and death are some of the effects of that divine sentence.

There was no sickness until after the fall of man. Physical illness and aging is linked to Adam's fall, but Jesus sealed a covenant of healing in His Body on the cross. So when we receive the Body and Blood of Christ, we have entered into the salvation covenant, which includes Christ's healing covenant for our bodies.

1 Peter 2:24 *He himself bore our sins in his body on the tree, so that we might die to sins and live for righteousness; by his wounds you have been healed.*

Matthew 8:16-17 *When evening came, many who were demon-possessed were brought to him, and he drove out the spirits with a word and healed all the sick. This was to fulfill what was spoken through the prophet Isaiah: "He took up our infirmities and bore our diseases."*

God established a different healing covenant with Israel in the wilderness. He said in Exodus that He was the Lord who healed them. His healing name is Jehovah Rapha, which identifies Himself as a healer for His people.

Exodus 15:26 *He said, "If you listen carefully to the voice of the Lord your God and do what is right in his eyes, if you pay attention to his commands and keep all his decrees, I will not bring on you any of the diseases I brought on the Egyptians, for I am the Lord, who heals you."*

But we have Jesus Christ, who was beaten across His back with a cat-o'-nine tails—a whip with nine leather straps embedded with glass and metal designed to inflict pain. His flesh was torn apart by the cat-o'-nine tails, and that is what caused rows of stripes on His back. (Are you thinking about what Matzo bread looks like?)

As long as you are here on this earth, your body will be subject to the divine sentence. Our natural bodies and brain cells are decaying every day. The Holy Communion is God's solution for you to offset the decay because it is **radically SUPERNATURAL!** God helps you offset the aging process and to walk in divine health. Every time you partake, you reverse the effects of the curse or divine judgment in your body.

The Meaning of Salvation

God is in the business of saving, not condemning. Salvation, in the most important sense, speaks of forgiveness of sins through repentance and faith in Jesus. But it also includes such blessings as divine healing, deliverance, preservation, and more.

The Greek word for salvation is *sozo*. It means "to preserve, heal and make whole." *Sozo*, another way to translate this word is "to be saved from the penalty of eternal judgment due to sins." Salvation is the daily process, or activity, of being whole.

Soteria, the other Greek word associated with salvation, is the identity of salvation. Basically, the word means that His sacrifice provided salvation, healing, deliverance, protection and all that Heaven has to offer. Everything is included in your salvation. It is a **complete work** of making a person whole in spirit, soul and body.

Do you see how simply putting these two words together you are able to get the whole picture? To be "saved" means to be saved, healed, delivered, preserved, protected, made prosperous and whole. The words "made whole" means to restore so that nothing is missing or broken.

I believe when Jesus said in **John 10:10** that "I have come that they may have life, and have it abundantly," He was not only speaking about your eternal future, but he was also speaking about your present life right here and now.

Thanks be to God that Jesus is the Spirit of Truth and *sozo* is an all-encompassing word! Praise God we are saved from hell and so much more! Aren't you thankful and grateful for the love of your Daddy God?

Keep His Word

Keep His Word and don't doubt it. Don't live below what God intended for you to live. You can train your Spirit man to rely on nothing but the Word of God. Based on the shed blood of Jesus, sickness does not belong in you. Become intimate with the truth—the Word of God. Your life will change dramatically. The devil has tried very hard to keep this truth from believers. But he is no match for those who believe in the power of the Lord's broken Body. And that is because he knows that he is no match for those who have *faith* in the power of Jesus' broken Body.

Revelation 3:8 *I know your deeds. See, I have placed before you an open door that no one can shut. I know that you have little strength, yet you have kept my word and have not denied my name.*

You only need faith for one thing, and that is to believe you are the righteousness of God in Christ Jesus, which causes every blessing you seek to come after you and overtake you.

Righteousness is a Gift

The scripture says it best.

2 Corinthians 5:21 *God made him who had no sin to be sin for us, so that in him we might become the righteousness of God.*

Romans 5:17 *For if, by the trespass of the one man, death reigned through that one man, how much more will those who receive God's abundant provision of grace and of the gift of righteousness reign in life through the one man, Jesus Christ!*

Jesus was not *just* whipped for your sins. The flesh was ripped from His Body for your sicknesses, pains and diseases also. Once you realize how much Jesus suffered so that your body can be made whole, you will be confident that partaking of His broken Body will bring healing to your body. It is a gift. If you have to work for it, or if it comes with conditions, then it is not a gift. God's gift of forgiveness and healing is unconditional.

God is such a merciful God. He has the perfect solution to sin and sickness. The simple act of eating a forbidden fruit by Adam brought disease and death to mankind. In contrast, God ordained the simple act of eating a crumb of bread to bring health and wholeness to His children—when done in remembrance of Him.

3 John 1:2 *Dear friend, I pray that you may enjoy good health and that all may go well with you, even as your soul is getting along well.*

As John the Apostle said, this is the perfect will of our most gracious heavenly Father who sent Jesus that we may share in His divine health. It is not because of how good we are but how good He is.

Praise God!

SECTION THREE

HIS DIVINE PLAN

They overcame him by the blood of the Lamb and by the word of their testimony; they did not love their lives so much as to shrink from death.

—Revelation 12:11

OUR GREAT JOY

The sufferings of Christ accomplished a divine plan to bring salvation and healing to those who would receive the new covenant. This impacted the body, soul, and spirit of everyone who has accepted the full atoning work of Jesus.

1 Thessalonians 5:23 *May God himself, the God of peace, sanctify you through and through. May your whole spirit, soul and body be kept blameless at the coming of our Lord Jesus Christ.*

Finished Work Prophesied

Isaiah prophesied that with His stripes we are healed. Isaiah looked **forward** to the atoning work of the Messiah. Peter looked **back** at the finished work of the cross and declared that by His stripes we were healed.

Isaiah 53:5 *But he was pierced for our transgressions, he was crushed for our iniquities; the punishment that brought us peace was on him, and by his wounds we are healed.*

1 Peter 2:24 *He himself bore our sins in his body on the tree, so that we might die to sins and live for righteousness; by his wounds you have been healed.*

Christ poured out His soul unto death. He made intercession for one thief who requested to be remembered when Jesus came in His kingdom.

Luke 23:39-43 *One of the criminals who hung there hurled insults at him: "Aren't you the Christ? Save yourself and us!"*
But the other criminal rebuked him. "Don't you fear God," he said, "since you are under the same sentence? We are punished justly, for we are getting what our deeds deserve. But this man has done nothing wrong."
Then he said, "Jesus, remember me when you come into your kingdom."
Jesus answered him, "I tell you the truth, today you will be with me in paradise."

Christ completed His redemptive work from the whipping post to the rugged post, the cross. The stripes on His back were for your physical healing. The thorns on His head were for your mental and emotional well-being. His suffering on the cross dealt a deathblow to sin and provided eternal life for you.

If Satan had know the full impact that Christ's death would have on his dark kingdom, he would had stopped His death, or should I say would have tried? God's ultimate purpose and plan could not be denied. Praise God!

Have you accepted God's salvation plan? If so, you can now rest in Him. God's rest celebrates His finished work. Those who enter into God's salvation can enter His rest by immediately abandoning any efforts to complement what God has perfected.

Hebrews 4: 9-11 *There remains, then, a Sabbath-rest for the people of God; for anyone who enters God's rest also rests from his own work, just as God did from his.*

Let us rejoice and praise God for His divine plan!

The Vine

In the Bible, the abundance of vines and vineyards is seen as an expression of God's favor. You can't have wine without the vine, and in the New Testament, Jesus is the Vine. In the Old Testament, scripture tells us that the nation of Israel was once God's flourishing transplanted vine and that the vine God transplanted was forsaken.

Psalm 80: 8-13 *You transplanted a vine out of Egypt; you drove out the nations and planted it.*

You cleared the ground for it, and it took root and filled the land.

The mountains were covered with its shade, the mighty cedars with its branches.

It sent out its boughs to the Sea, its shoots as far as the River.

Why have you broken down its walls so that all who pass by pick its grapes?

Boars from the forest ravage it, and insects from the fields feed on it.

Isaiah 5:1-7 *I will sing for the one I love a song about his vineyard: My loved one had a vineyard on a fertile hillside. He dug it up and cleared it of stones and planted it with the choicest vines. He built a watchtower in it and cut out a winepress as well. Then he looked for a crop of good grapes, but it yielded only bad fruit.*

"Now you dwellers in Jerusalem and men of Judah, judge between me and my vineyard. What more could have been done for my vineyard than I have done for it? When I looked for good grapes, why did it yield only bad? Now I will tell you what I am going to do to my vineyard:

I will take away its hedge, and it will be destroyed; I will break down its wall, and it will be trampled. I will make it a wasteland, neither pruned nor cultivated, and briers and thorns will grow there. I will command the clouds not to rain on it."

The vineyard of the Lord Almighty is the house of Israel, and the men of Judah are the garden of his delight. And he looked for justice, but saw bloodshed; for righteousness, but heard cries of distress.

Israel was planted a "choice vine" but became a "wild vine."

Jeremiah 2:21 *I had planted you like a choice vine of sound and reliable stock. How then did you turn against me into a corrupt, wild vine?*

The new wine spoken of in the Old Testament is Jesus, the anointing of God to release the abundance of God's life in the lives of His people.

Jeremiah 31:12 *They will come and shout for joy on the heights of Zion; they will rejoice in the bounty of the LORD— the grain, the new wine and the oil, the young of the flocks and herds. They will be like a well-watered garden, and they will sorrow no more.*

Psalm 104: 14-15 *He makes grass grow for the cattle, and plants for man to cultivate—bringing forth food from the earth; wine that gladdens the heart of man, oil to make his face shine, and bread that sustains his hearts.*

God gives you strength to stand against the enemy while walking in abundance here on earth. He wants you to have the fullness of all His blessings in every season. The Spirit of God wants to release a fresh supply of New Wine to His Body of believers, His Church. With God, you're always in season!

The New Wine

Stomping is the first step in the process of winemaking. The grape juice is found in the middle of the grape while yeast grows on the outside of the grape skin. The yeast is what produces fermentation. When grapes are stomped, the grape skin is broken and the yeast mixes with the juice and new wine comes forth.

Matthew 9:16-17 *No one sews a patch of unshrunk cloth on an old garment, for the patch will pull away from the garment, making the tear worse. Neither do men pour new* *wine into old wineskins. If they do, the skins will burst, the wine will run our and the wineskins will be ruined. No, they pour new wine into new wineskins, and both are preserved.*

Jesus brings a newness that cannot be confined inside old form. Often when God gives us a vision, our flesh grabs a hold of it and tries to make it happen using our self-gratifying energy, however, our flesh cannot please God. He has to put our desires and ambitions into the winepress and stomp on them until our flesh lets go.

Is this not a picture of how God deals with our flesh? Is it not also a picture of Christ and what He did for you?

In order to come into a place of God's blessing, we may have to experience the death of a vision. For example, Abraham waited twenty-five years before he recognized his inability to make God's promise materialize. God allowed David to be hunted by Saul until David finally trusted his future entirely to God. Moses was in a position to set Israel free, but he had retreat into the desert before he was allowed to fulfill his destiny.

God will allow your vision to be stomped. He will wait for it to die and then He will resurrect it by supernatural power. God always works through life, death and resurrection. If all your dreams and hopes seemed to have died, then you are in a season of resurrection. God will release His New Wine in you.

God wants you to shift from ambition to submission. He wants you to go from trying to trusting. He wants you to walk away from your old ways, plans and mindsets. He wants you to give up the old attitude of "I can make it happen" and adopt the new attitude of "God will make it happen!"

The New Wine of the His Spirit will flow when this shifting takes place. If you find yourself in the winepress, stop reaching back for the old and familiar. Don't rely on your ability to make "it" happen. Instead, declare God's Word by faith. Trust God to allow all that He has for you.

Bruising and Breaking

Unless the skin of the grape is broken, it will end up a raisin. Think about it. Before we can experience the New Wine, we must be broken and bruised. Don't resist the stomping. We cannot avoid trials in our lifetime. We are going to go *through* them. How we react to adversity is what matters.

John 16:33 *Christ said, "I have told you these things, so that in me you may have peace. In this world you will have trouble. But take heart! I have overcome the world."*

When you go *through* the fire, or what feels like a fiery trial, choose to allow God to refine you. Fire separates the foreign and impure materials from gold while it loses nothing of its nature, weight, color, or any other property. The trials we experience in this life are like fire. They refine and prove our faith to be genuine.

1 Peter 1:6-7 *In this you greatly rejoice, though now for a little while you may have had to suffer grief in all kinds of* *trials. These have come so that the proven genuineness of your faith—of greater worth than gold, which perishes even though refined by fire—may result in praise, glory and honor when Jesus Christ is revealed.*

Scripture teaches us that when compared to the eternal glory one receives for suffering, our trials will be for a little while. We rejoice in salvation, but once in awhile, it is needful for you to go *through* temptations so that your faith can be tested. Remember, God rewards genuine faith.

2 Corinthians 4:16-18 *Therefore we do not lose heart. Though outwardly we are wasting away, yet inwardly we are being renewed day by day. For our light and momentary troubles are achieving for us an eternal glory that far outweighs them all. So we fix our eyes not on what is seen, but on what is unseen, since what is seen is temporary, but what is unseen is eternal.*

Do not strive for things that are seen, for they are not worthy of the pursuit of an immortal soul. They are temporal. Strive for things that are not seen and eternal. These are the important things in life.

When your view of Daddy God is accurate, you will welcome the stomping for New Wine. The opposite is also true. An old way of thinking or a wrong perception of God will decrease intimacy when you commune with Him. Think of it this way. The new wineskin represents the foundation of your thinking, which leads to your perception of God.

John 6:32-35 *Jesus said to them, "I tell you the truth, it is not Moses who has given you the bread from heaven, but it is my Father who give you the true bread from heaven. For the* *bread of God is he who comes down from heaven and gives life to the world." "Sir," they said, "from now on give us this bread." Then Jesus declared, "I am the bread of life."*

Embrace the Bread from heaven and the New Wine of His presence with a right perspective of God's nature. His presence will produce love, joy, and peace resulting in a pure devotion to God and His purpose.

Freedom, Joy, Restoration

God declares that you can have freedom in Him right now. He brings the joy that will restore your soul TODAY! He identifies with your pain and suffering. He knows what it is like to suffer at the hands of others, yet He proclaims joy and strength. God provides, as He always does. He gives us a garment of praise instead of a spirit of despair. God cares about every tear you shed.

Isaiah 61:3 *...and provide for those who grieve in Zion—to bestow on them a crown of beauty instead of ashes, the oil of joy instead of mourning, and a garment of praise instead of a spirit of despair. They will be called oaks of righteousness, a planting of the Lord for the display of his splendor.*

This means that all who mourn will be given a beautiful tiara instead of the ashes typically thrown on the head while mourning. The oil of gladness denotes that which expresses joy and happiness. And to top it off, God gives us a garment that expresses praise and gratitude instead of a spirit of heaviness or a burdened heart.

Praise God! We can display His splendor! That is a humbling yet gratifying thought. What an awesome privilege, but God offers us even more. God offers us restoration. He will restore that which was taken from us. He is the One who can restore what the enemy has taken.

Joel 2:25 *"I will repay you for the years the locusts have eaten—the great locust and the young locust, the other locusts and the locust swarm—my great army that I sent among you."*

Bible Study

You don't always feel like getting in the Word when you are going through your greatest trial, but *do it anyway*! Was I totally focused while going through my health challenges? No, not by any stretch of the imagination, but I knew to do what was in my best interest and I did it.

Choosing to stay close to God and getting into His Word is a choice you have to make. Only you can make the decision for yourself. I decided to choose the Bible study *Experiencing God* by Henry Blackaby during my struggles. This study truly brought me into the presence of God, which is why I highly recommend it to everyone no matter where they are on their walk with the Lord.

My experience drove home the truth of how important it is to position myself to hear the Lord. I want to step out into His will in obedience because this is where I will see His power manifested. I learned to turn what could have become a stumbling block, into a stepping-stone for personal growth. I am stronger because I stood on the promises of God. I stood on the promises of God because I studied them in the Bible. I'm stronger because my faith grew as a result of spending time studying my Bible.

Perseverance

On your journey to the place where God wants to lead you, remember to study those stumbling blocks so you can turn them into steppingstones of faith. Don't make the mistake of thinking trials will make you stronger. Trials come to test your faith. And if your faith is not fighting back, you are not winning. You pass the test of faith by overcoming each trial, not by keeping the trial. God permits the trials to come so that you will have the opportunity to exercise your faith and become stronger.

Trials can be beneficial. This is why we count it all joy when we face trials of many kinds; the testing of our faith develops perseverance. Perseverance must finish its work so that we will be mature and complete, not lacking any good thing.

By the way, it is not my intent to minimize your pain. My encouragement to you is to try to see struggles as challenges. Try to learn and grow closer to God in all circumstances.

James 1:2-4 *Consider it pure joy, my brothers, whenever you face trials of many kinds, because you know that the testing of your faith develops perseverance. Perseverance must finish its works so that you may be mature and complete, not lacking anything.*

FORGIVENESS

> *To be a Christian means to forgive the inexcusable because God has forgiven the inexcusable in you."*
>
> —C. S. Lewis

Obedience

Obedience to the Word includes not only fully understanding and participating in Communion, but it also includes releasing anyone who has harmed you physically, emotionally or spiritually. This is how we judge ourselves at the Lord's Table, by examining our relationship with both God and man.

Sometimes people suffer from poor health not because of what they eat, but they suffer from what is eating at them. Resentment, hate, grudges, jealousy, and unforgiveness are all attitudes that need to go. Unforgiveness can make people physically ill. Often, holding grudges makes people emotionally sick. And in every case, unforgiveness always causes spiritual suffering.

Ask yourself if you are harboring any ill will, resentment or grudges. If so, can you let them go out without delay? I hope so. They do nothing but consume you and destroy your life.

Forgiveness for Your Sake

Forgiveness is for your own sake, not the sake of the one who hurt you. It means releasing the pain from your power to God's power. When you don't forgive, it is telling God that you don't trust Him to handle the situation, inferring that you could do a better job. It is an insult to the God of the universe. Agree with God over the matter because He has extended His mercy to you. Surrender the situation and all the repercussions as well as the hurtful person to Him.

2 Corinthians 2:10-11 *If you forgive anyone, I also forgive. And what I have forgiven—I have forgiven in the sight of Christ for your sake, in order that Satan might not outwit us. For we are not unaware of his schemes.*

God's Word not only tells you what is wrong but also how to correct it. He says to fill your mind with attitudes of goodwill, forgiveness, faith, love and a spirit that is unshakable. Every time you feel anger say, "It isn't worth it to spend $5,000 worth of emotion on a five-cent irritation."

Pray for the one who has hurt you. Pray specifically for the person who has hurt you. Sometimes you may have to pray for quite a while to get that result. You need to pray until the grievance leaves and peace comes, even if it is 777 times. Pray it out of your system. Speak out forgiveness of your heart and eventually your heart will follow and catch up with the confession of your mouth.

This is guaranteed to work, so you can go ahead and praise God for His greatness and faithfulness. Love that forgives does not operate from an earthly agenda. Trust God, not man.

Don't Grow Weary

Don't give in and let discouragement defeat you. If your life circumstances seem hopeless, stand up and believe. Wrap your arms of faith around His promise.

Hebrews 10:23 *Let us hold unswervingly to the hope we profess, for he who promised is faithful.*

Galatians 6:9 *Let us not become weary in doing good, for at the proper time we will reap a harvest if we do not give up.*

Satan will take advantage of every Christian's weaknesses and failures. He wants to get into your life and cause your downfall by creating unforgiveness, which leads to a stubborn root of bitterness. This is at the top of Satan's list. Unforgiveness and hardness of heart—it does great harm to the cause of Christ.

Matthew 5:43-45 *"You have heard that it was said, 'Love your neighbor and hate your enemy.' But I tell you: love your enemies and pray for those who persecute you, that you may be sons of your Father in heaven."*

The list is pretty simple.

Here it is:

Love your enemies.

Bless them that curse you.

Do good to those who hate you.

Pray for your persecutors.

Jesus tells us to abide in His love. Abiding in His love is like being a child in the womb. I once heard someone say that we are to place our ear against the chest of the Savior so that, when troubled times come, we can hear the steady pulse of the boundless love of Him who holds us close. You may not know what will happen next, but you can know and trust His loving embrace now and forever.

John 15:9 *"As the Father has loved me, so have I loved you. Now remain in my love.*

SUFFERING

Blessed is any weight, however overwhelming, which God has been so good as to fasten with His own Hand upon our shoulder.

—*F. W. Faber*

No Tear is Wasted

You may have suffered a great loss. Your future may have been changed in ways you didn't desire or deserve. Your pain is real just like my pain was real. But you should know that when your heart is breaking, God's promises aren't. You can rest assured that when you cry, no tear is wasted. The New Living Translation Bible says it this way.

Psalm 56: 8 *You keep track of all my sorrows. You have collected all my tears in your bottle. You have recorded each one in your book.*

God is adding to the story of your life. Allow Him to use those tears. Suffering, by the way, does not come from God. It comes from the devil. Your enemy, the devil, prowls around like a roaring lion looking for someone to devour. Satan brought all kinds of suffering to the early church and he still brings suffering to many faithful believers today.

Unfortunately, many Christians think they are supposed to embrace suffering, because they think it is from God. Christians should not embrace or accept suffering. Quite the opposite is true. We should resist suffering by standing firm in faith.

Suffering and trials may come, but they are not to stay.

1 Peter 1: 6-7 *In this you greatly rejoice, though now for a little while, you may have had to suffer grief in all kinds of trials. These have come so that your faith—of greater worth than gold, which perishes even though refined by fire—may be proven genuine and result in praise, glory and honor when Jesus Christ is revealed.*

Enemy Attacks

The enemy will cause you to think, is it really God's will for me to be healed? And the answer is, of course it is God's will for you to be healed. God's Word says He is willing.

Matthew 8:1-3 *When he came down from the mountainside, large crowds followed him. A man with leprosy came and knelt before him and said, "Lord, if you are willing, you can make me clean."*
Jesus reached out his hand and touched the man. "I am willing," he said. "Be clean!" Immediately he was cured of his leprosy.

The enemy will bring an old sin to your mind, or he will use critics to remind you of your past. Sometimes, it's your own family who become your worst critics. But the enemy is a thief, liar and murderer. He is out to kill, steal and destroy.

He does not like to lose and will take every chance to take back his territory and rob you of your blessing.

John 10:10 *The thief comes only to steal and kill and destroy; I have come that they may have life, and have it to the full.*

What brings us victory? Our faith. Faith brings us victory. But remember, before every victory there has to be a battle. Some people think the victorious life is a life without battles, but this is not true. You can't say you won when you didn't have an opponent. And this is important because scripture tell us to testify what the Lord has done for us.

Revelation 12:11 *They triumphed over him by the blood of the Lamb and by the word of their testimony; they did not love their lives so much as to shrink from death.*

Remember, we must profess our faith in Christ's ability to keep our body, soul and spirit whole. This is a powerful principal to use when we are disabling the works of the enemy.

Shattered Dreams

Have your dreams ever been shattered? Has hurt ever blinded you to the good that God was doing? If so, I can relate. When my dreams went from delightful thoughts to disappointment, I decided to study the life of Joseph and was encouraged to press on. I didn't fully understood what it meant to persevere until after I had gone through the pain.

Joseph's life story gives us a good picture of brokenness. I know I was blessed when I read it.

Even though Joseph's brothers intended for him to die, he did not die at the hands of his brothers. He lived to play a part in God's divine plan. Joseph was destined to do kingdom work. Many people and animals were spared during the seven years of famine because of Joseph's faithful spirit.

Genesis 50:20 *You intended to harm me, but God intended it for good to accomplish what is now being done, the saving of many lives.*

In all the afflictions and rejection Joseph experienced, he never despaired. Instead, he kept his attention on God. Throughout his life, Joseph allowed God to crush him and break his temporal life so that the product of his brokenness could bless others.

Only a spirit-filled Joseph could truly say to his brothers, "God used your evil plot against me for good."

IN HIS PRESENCE

Overheard in an Orchard

Said the Robin to the Sparrow;
 "I should really like to know
Why these anxious human beings
 Rush about and worry so?"
Said the Sparrow to the Robin:
 Friend, I think that it must be
That they have no Heavenly Father
 Such as cares for you and me."

—Elizabeth Cheney

Priorities

If Satan has his demons and God has His army of redeemers, then we, as believers must arm ourselves with discernment. We must make discernment a priority.

Throughout the centuries, the world has seen Christianity in various, sometimes awful ways. It is up to us, the body of Christ, to reveal the ***true*** Christ as He manifests Himself through His body of believers. In order to do this, we must have our priorities straight. We must strive to be the disciples Christ actually wants to represent Him on earth. We must possess the mind of Christ so that we can pursue His kingdom work in a manner that truly glorifies Him.

Consider the following warning. Don't live in the past. This only leads to regret and bitterness. If you have repented, God's grace will cover past sins and failings. Allow your past to be pruned away; instead of being a bitter drink offering, you will become a sweet drink offering to the Lord. The pruning process brings about the new you.

Press in and draw closer to your Daddy God where there is a place of overwhelming life and joy. Allow His new wine to fill you. New wine is a sign of God's presence dwelling within you. It brings with it the fullness of God's security and provision. Rejoice, new wine is part of the bounty of the Lord!

However, it is still wise to ask God to show you any little foxes that may be trying to crush the vine, the one that brings forth the new wine and expands your garden. Ask Him to give you the first fruits of increase so your vats will run over with the new wine. Your Daddy God desires to come into your vineyard and reveal to you the prophetic fruit He is going to bring forth in your future. It's all about entering into your promised inheritance.

Also, don't live focused on what lies ahead in your future. Instead, know that you have a good future. Ask your Daddy God for revelation for the building plan for your future. Ask for keys to unlock the kingdom of God within you, then unlock the door of hope and open it. This is where heaven and earth agree.

Make the following priorities in your life:

Seek first His kingdom and righteousness.

Seek His wisdom, knowledge and understanding.

Love God, yourself, family and others.

Seek health and wholeness.

Be anxious for nothing.

Seek all your Daddy God has for you.

Seek Him first and all of the rest will fall into place.

Matthew 6:33 *Seek first his kingdom and his righteousness and all these things will be given to you as well.*

Flow in God's Power

Remember, the spirit of the antichrist denies the finished work of Christ. It is a hindrance to move in God's power. It keeps you bound in a "work mentality." Guilt and shame will also hinder the move of the spirit and will keep you from flowing in the supernatural. Be aware that perfectionism is connected to legalism and will also keep you from flowing in God's power.

You are created in the image of Christ, washed white as snow in His Blood and God wants to use you, therefore, your spirit is perfect, clothed with His righteousness. With that in mind, seek to experience God's power. Be hungry for the supernatural. Seek to know the power of the resurrection. Have the mind of Christ and see beyond what you can see in the natural.

Philippians 3:8-10 *What is more, I consider everything a lost compared to the surpassing greatness of knowing Christ Jesus my Lord, for whose sake I have lost all things. I consider them rubbish, that I may gain Christ and be found in him, not having a righteousness of my own that comes from the law, but that which is through faith in Christ—the righteousness that comes from God and is by faith. I want to know Christ—yes, to know the power of his resurrection and participation in his sufferings, becoming like him in his death,...*

Receive your blessings. Declare that any premature aging or stiffness will break from you and become a new wineskin. Declare that which has been scattered will come back together into a new structure. Let go of any old method that is operating in your life. Allow the old season to end and the new season to begin.

Heaven was opened to man since the veil came down. Press *through* and touch Jesus in your weakness. Plead the Body and the Blood of Jesus over you and the enemy must bow down and back away. He has no authority and cannot pass through what His Body and the Blood cover.

Revel in your dinner with your Daddy God. Take great pleasure and delight as you dance and celebrate in His presence. This is the only dinner you will ever celebrate that brings you total wholeness. Be blessed!

You are His Presence in the World

As a believer, you are Christ to the world. Those you come in contact with should experience Christ when they meet you. It is no longer you who lives but Christ in you. I am certain you have heard someone say before, "We should preach and teach everywhere we go but only use words when absolutely necessary." Why is that said so often? It's easy—Christ is the Word that became flesh. Be Jesus to people!

It would be good to memorize this scripture:

Galatians 2:20 *I have been crucified with Christ and I no longer live, but Christ lives in me. The life I now live in the body, I live by faith in the Son of God, who loved me and gave himself for me.*

You should ingest the Word of God so that by absorbing (or digesting) His life, He can be formed in you. Ingestion without digestion causes the uncomfortable sensation of being full. Therefore, after ingesting His Word, digest the full meal of His presence, and you will conform to His image. It's both amazing and true.

People, since before Christ was born, have been full of religion, but religion will never satisfy the longing of the soul. Jesus wants you to be filled with Him, *not* religion. You are Christ to all you come in contact with because His Word becomes flesh as you reveal Jesus to the world around you. You are His Body on earth.

Listen to Jesus as He prays for us:

John 17:20-23 *My prayer is not for them alone. I pray also for those who will believe in me through their message, that all of them may be one, Father, just as you are in me and I am in you. May they also be in us so that the world may believe that you have sent me. I have given them the glory that you gave me, that they may be one as we are one: I in them and you in me. May they may be brought to complete unity to let the world will know that you sent me and have loved them even as you have loved me.*

This is true unity between the Bride of Christ and the Bridegroom, Jesus. When you come to His table to commune with Him, it is impossible to separate the unity between you and Him. The angel in **Revelation 19:9** says to the apostle John, *"Write: Blessed are those who are invited to the wedding supper of the Lamb!"*

When you commune with God, have dinner with Him, you will experience His presence every time! As an heir of the King of Kings and Lord of Lords, you can move in the fullness of God's resurrection power in your daily life. Just ask the Holy Spirit to grant unto you greater revelation of what being His son or daughter really means.

John 1:14 *The Word became flesh and made his dwelling among us. We have seen his glory, the glory of the one and only Son, who came from the Father, full of grace and truth.*

It is a fact—Almighty God is, truly, your Daddy God.

Spiritual Retreats

Attending a spiritual retreat means a great deal to me. I experienced the Walk to Emmaus retreat about fifteen years ago. Today, I am active in The Walk to Emmaus and as well as Tres Dias. I suspect anyone you talk to who has attended a spiritual retreat will speak of only good things as well as how deeply the Lord blessed them as a result. Let me explain.

Walk to Emmaus

What is the walk to Emmaus? The walk to Emmaus is an experience of Christian spiritual renewal and formation that begins with a three-day short course in Christianity. It is an opportunity to meet Jesus Christ in a new way as God's grace and love is revealed to you through other believers.

The Walk to Emmaus experience begins with the prayerful discernment and invitation from a sponsor. After one accepts this invitation they complete an application. The Emmaus leaders prayerfully consider each applicant and in God's time, the person is invited to attend a three-day experience of New Testament Christianity as a lifestyle.

Following the three-day experience, participants are joined in small groups to support each other in their ongoing walk with Christ. Through the formational process of accountable discipleship in small groups and participation in the Emmaus community, each participant's individual gifts and servant-leadership skills are developed for use in the local church and its mission. Participants are encouraged to find ways to live out their individual call to discipleship in their home, church, and community.

The objective of Emmaus is to inspire, challenge, and equip the local church members for Christian action in their homes, churches, communities and places of work. Emmaus lifts up a way for our grace-filled lives to be lived and shared with others.

What is Tres Dias? Tres Dias is an inter-denominational three-day weekend retreat. The focus of the weekend is "God's unmerited love." The weekend is designed to show the "agape" type love that God pours out on us. This is love that is unconditional, unmerited, and for which the only true response can be love in return. The goal is to empower Christians to become leaders within their families, their small groups, churches and communities.

What Happened on the Road to Emmaus?

Here's how the story starts out:

Luke 24:13-35 *Now that same day two of them were going to a village called Emmaus, about seven miles from Jerusalem. They were talking with each other about everything that had happened. As they talked and discussed these things with each other, Jesus himself came up and walked along with them; but they were kept from recognizing him.*
    He asked them, "What are you discussing together as you walk along?"
    They stood still, their faces downcast. One of them, named Cleopas, asked him, "Are you the only one visiting Jerusalem

who does not know the things that have happened there in these days?"

"What things?" he asked.

"About Jesus of Nazareth," they replied. "He was a prophet, powerful in word and deed before God and all the people. The chief priests and our rulers handed him over to be sentenced to death, and they crucified him; but we had hoped that he was the one who was going to redeem Israel. And what is more, it is the third day since all this took place. In addition, some of our women amazed us. They went to the tomb early this morning but didn't find his body. They came and told us that they had seen a vision of angels, who said he was alive. Then some of our companions went to the tomb and found it just as the women had said, but they did not see."

He said to them, "How foolish you are, and how slow of heart to believe all that the prophets have spoken! Did not Christ have to suffer these things and then enter his glory?" And beginning with Moses and all the Prophets, he explained to them what was said in all the Scriptures concerning himself.

As they approached the village to which they were going, Jesus continued on as if he were going farther. But they urged him strongly, "Stay with us, for it is nearly evening; the day is almost over." So he went in to stay with them.

When he was at the table with them, he took bread, gave thanks, broke it and began to give it to them. Then their eyes were opened and they recognized him, and he disappeared from their sight. They asked each other "Were not our hearts burning within us while he talked with us on the road and opened the Scriptures to us?"

They got up and returned at once to Jerusalem. There they found the Eleven and those with them, assembled together and saying, "It is true! The Lord has risen and has appeared to Simon." Then the two told what had happened on the way, and how Jesus was recognized by them when he broke the bread.

The story gets exciting when Jesus' disciples finally recognize Him.

Luke 24: 36-49 *While they were still talking about this, Jesus himself stood among them and said to them, "Peace be with you."*

They were startled and frightened, thinking they saw a ghost. He said to them, "Why are you troubled, and why do doubts rise in your minds? Look at my hands and my feet. It is I myself! Touch me and see; a ghost does not have flesh and bones, as you see I have."

When he had said this, he showed them his hands and feet. And while they still did not believe it because of joy and amazement, he asked them, "Do you have anything here to eat?" They gave him a piece of broiled fish, and he took it and ate it in their presence.

He said to them, "This is what I told you while I was still with you: Everything must be fulfilled that is written about me in the Law of Moses, the Prophets and the Psalms."

Then he opened their minds so they could understand the Scriptures. He told them, "This is what is written: The Christ will suffer and rise from the dead on the third day, and repentance for the forgiveness of sins will be preached in his name to all nations, beginning at Jerusalem. You are witnesses of these things. I am going to send you what my Father has promised; but stay in the city until you have been clothed with power from on high."

The high point of the story comes with the ascension of Jesus into heaven.

Luke 24: 50-52 *When he had led them out to the vicinity of Bethany, he lifted up his hands and blessed them. While he was blessing them, he left them and was taken up into heaven. Then they worshiped him and returned to Jerusalem with great joy.*

As I studied these Scriptures, verses 30 and 31 really jumped out at me. *When he was at the table with them, he took break, gave thanks, broke it and began to give it to them. Then their eyes were opened and they recognized him...*

They had Communion! The similarity of the institution of the Lord's Supper in Matthew 26:26 indicates to me that Jesus celebrated it here to open their eyes and prove to them that He was no stranger after all. They shared the Lord's Supper with Jesus and their eyes were opened and at that very moment they recognized Jesus.

Isn't this what this book is all about—opening your eyes as you commune with your Daddy God through the broken Body and Blood of Jesus?

My Prayer for You

Excuse me. I must stop and pray.

> *Oh dear Daddy God, please open the eyes of each person who places this book in their hands. Open their eyes and let them recognize you.*
> *Dear readers, may you not be a stranger to God any more. I pray that this message reaches the very depths of your spirit for a deeper revelation of Communion. May your eyes be opened and may you receive the truth and be blessed by this revelation. I pray that you come and dine with your Daddy God and receive all His wonderful blessings as you commune with Him.*
> *May the Lord help you to comprehend the journey you are on with Him. May the Lord help you recognize His perspective and give you a view from above the clouds. May you focus on the hope and love-filled*

amazing things He pours out as a result of gaining revelation of His complete and expanded view. May you understand His heart, wisdom and healing. As you walk with him, may you gain understanding of what you may have forgotten or missed. My prayer for you, dear readers, is that you desire to represent Him accurately and be a portal of hope to others.

Lastly, may you live in the middle of His resurrection power, calling His Word to come forth and commanding His Word to become active, for His Word is alive and eternal. And most of all, may you find answers, all of which are available and found in His presence. In Jesus' Name, AMEN!

FINAL THOUGHTS

You are identified with Christ in all He is, was, or will be. Your enemy may be stubborn and resist you, but your will is set—you are going to win and you literally charge on the enemy in that all-conquering Name of Jesus Christ. The enemy may stand for a time, but he must yield.

—E. W. Kenyon

Daddy God Really Is...

Your Daddy God *really* is a gracious and merciful Savior. You need to know the truth about Who He is, and what you believe about God must be based on the solid foundation of God's Word. To know this truth, you can't go by feelings, circumstances or what you may have heard or been taught by someone else. You have to go to the source.

Please don't live with a distorted perception of God when you can get in His Word and see for yourself what the Bible says about Him. Don't be fearful of Him. Go to Him and receive His love, grace and forgiveness. Allow Him to come into your situation. He desires to dine with you and have an intimate relationship with you.

Don't even take my word for it. There are a lot of Scriptures in this book. Meditate on them and ask Him to reveal to you what He desires to speak. He longs to hear from you, and yes, you can hear from Him. He will make His message clear to you because He wants you to experience His Resurrection power.

Watch as He manifests Himself in your life and His Kingdom starts to direct your life. Be led by His Spirit. Get ready for an encounter with your Daddy God.

Yes, **REALLY,** God is who He says He is.
Yes, **REALLY,** God is love.
Yes, **REALLY,** His Word is true.
Yes, **REALLY,** He is your Source.
Yes, **REALLY,** you should believe Him.
Yes, **REALLY,** choose Him.
Yes, **REALLY,** He is gracious.
Yes, **REALLY,** He is merciful.
Yes, **REALLY,** He loves you.
Yes, **REALLY,** He is compassionate.
Yes, **REALLY,** He is amazing.
Yes, **REALLY,** He is in control.
Yes, **REALLY,** you matter to Him.
Yes, **REALLY,** He is all-powerful.
Yes, **REALLY,** He hears your prayers.
Yes, **REALLY,** He is your refuge.
Yes, **REALLY,** you are perfect in His sight.
Yes, **REALLY,** it is a finished work.
Yes, **REALLY,** you are blessed.
Yes, **REALLY**, you are the righteousness of Christ.
Yes, **REALLY,** His Covenant is a guarantee.
Yes, **REALLY,** God favors you.
Yes, **REALLY,** His Word says He will prosper you.

Yes, **REALLY,** God gives you preferential treatment.
Yes **REALLY,** believing is receiving.
Yes, **REALLY,** God is not judging you.
Yes, **REALLY,** God is trustworthy.
Yes, **REALLY,** God is your strength.
Yes, **REALLY,** He is willing.
Yes, **REALLY,** you can stand on His promises.
Yes, **REALLY,** His Body and Blood heals and forgives.
Yes, **REALLY,** He protects.
Yes, **REALLY,** He favors you.
Yes, **REALLY,** He SAVES.
Yes, **REALLY,** He HEALS
Yes, **REALLY**, He FORGIVES.
Yes, **REALLY,** He is your DADDY GOD.

And yes, you are really His favorite. Yes, really, I mean really, as in Your Daddy God truly desires to have dinner with you. **REALLY!!!!!!!**

EPILOGUE

Will you join me in seeking the truth of the Lord's grace and rest in His finished work? Choose to focus on Christ's perfect obedience and how His obedience at Calvary makes us righteous, whole, healthy, favored and complete.

The truth is that Jesus came for us as one of us. He died for us, and as one of us. He received the approval of Daddy God for us, as one of us. He came as our representative, and if that were not enough, Daddy God tells us in His Word that we are His Beloved. Daddy God sees us as His Beloved because He has made us acceptable through Jesus. He wants us to wake up each day knowing that we are His Beloved treasure. We are unconditionally loved and approved.

The more we receive this in our spirit, the more we can expect good things to happen in our lives. We can expect to be healthy and whole when we realize that we are the objects of our Daddy God's love. Be confident that we will win every fight in life. We are one with the Lord and are God-like here on earth.

Take every opportunity to dine with your Daddy God and receive what is available and rightfully yours so that you can walk rightly connected with Daddy God.

I wanted to end with a prayer of salvation since this is where your journey begins, that is, if you haven't already prayed this prayer of salvation. So, please, if you haven't done so already, pray this prayer to receive all that Jesus has done for you. Invite Him to be your Lord and Savior.

> *Lord Jesus, thank you for loving me and dying for me on the cross at Calvary. Your Blood washes me clean of every sin. I receive you as Lord and Savior, now and forever. I believe you died for my sins and rose from the dead and are alive today. Because of Your finished work, I am now a beloved child of my Daddy God and heaven is my eternal home. I trust you and will follow you. Thank you for filling me with peace and joy.*
>
> *In Jesus' name, Amen.*

John 3:16 *For God so loved the world that he gave his one and only Son, that whoever believes in him shall not perish but have eternal life.*

And finally, here's the how-to of celebrating communion. This is the prayer you should pray from your heart, not your head:

The Body:

Thank you Jesus, for your broken Body. Thank you for bearing my symptoms and sicknesses at the cross so that I may have your health and wholeness. I declare that by the beating you accepted and the stripes on your back, I am completely healed. I believe and I receive your resurrection life in my body today.

Eat the bread.

The Blood:

Thank You Jesus, for your Blood that has washed me whiter than snow. Your Blood has brought me forgiveness and made me righteous forever. As I drink, I celebrate and participate in the inheritance of the righteous, which includes preservation, healing, wholeness and all your blessings.

Drink the wine.

In Christ,
Joye W. Letourneau

ABOUT THE AUTHOR

Rachel Strickland Photography

Joye W. has walked victoriously through fire and water without burning or drowning, meaning she has personally experienced divine healing. She not only experienced healing, but she also experienced the divine Healer and His resurrection power. Over the years, she has studied the Scriptures on the subject of healing and thoughtfully documented her journey. She shares her experience in her first book, *Walking Through the C Word* by Joye W.

In her books, Joye captures just how big God is. You can do the same as you join her on this journey to healing and wholeness that has been provided for all believers at the cross of Calvary in the Body of Jesus Christ. By the way, Joye has been cancer-free for over 15 years!

Dinner with My Daddy God is available on Amazon in both soft cover and Kindle. To order multiple copies, please contact the author by email. j.letourneau901@comcast.net.

www.ingramcontent.com/pod-product-compliance
Lightning Source LLC
Chambersburg PA
CBHW061656040126
42446CB00010B/1773